S0-AXN-872

SPOTLIGHT

DISCARDED

PENNSYLVANIA DUTCH COUNTRY

ANNA DUBROVSKY

Contents

PENNSYLVANIA DUTCH COUNTRY

PENNSYLVANIA DUTCH COUNTRY

The portion of the state referred to as Pennsylvania Dutch Country has no blockbuster cities. Its largest, Reading, has a mere 80,000 residents. And yet it receives more visitors than Philadelphia, more visitors than Pittsburgh—more visitors than any other region in the state. Part of the reason is the public's fascination with the Amish, whose way of life is in sharp contrast to the average American's. Lancaster County, the most popular destination in Dutch Country, boasts the largest concentration of Amish in the world. Their use of horse-drawn buggies, adherence to strict dress codes, and rejection of technologies including television and computers makes them exotic. A casual drive through Lancaster County's fertile farmlands has a safari-esque quality. ("Look, honey, buggy at 3 o'clock!") Unlike giraffes and

elephants, the Amish take offense to being photographed, so resist the temptation to aim your camera at the farmer working his fields with mule-drawn equipment, the children driving a pony cart, or the women selling their pies and preserves at a market stand.

There's more to the region's allure than the Amish experience. Less than 40 miles from the heart of Amish country is the town of Hershey, the product of one chocolatier's expansive vision. Few places offer as high a concentration of family-friendly attractions as the "Sweetest Place on Earth." In the southern part of Pennsylvania Dutch Country is the town of Gettysburg, site of the Civil War's bloodiest battle and President Abraham Lincoln's most memorable speech. The place throbs with history—and not just on days when it's awash

HIGHLIGHTS

◖ **Amish Attractions:** If you learned everything you know about the Amish from the movie *Witness*, you've got a lot to learn. Get schooled at Plain & Fancy Farm, the Amish Farm and House, or the Mennonite Information Center (page 12).

◖ **Strasburg Rail Road** and the **Railroad Museum of Pennsylvania:** The nation's oldest operating short-line railroad and the state's official train museum are across-the-street neighbors in "Train Town USA" (page 22).

◖ **Air Museums:** With two aviation museums within 20 miles of each other, greater Reading could well be called "Plane Town USA." Take to the skies in an antique plane, or take a trip back in time during the Mid-Atlantic Air Museum's World War II Weekend (page 57).

◖ **Hawk Mountain Sanctuary:** Some 20,000 hawks, eagles, and falcons soar past this raptor sanctuary on their southward journeys. The sight is awe-inspiring and the hiking terrific (page 59).

◖ **The Hershey Story:** One of Pennsylvania's newest museums, The Hershey Story offers hands-on experience in chocolate-making (page 70).

◖ **Hersheypark:** Hershey's century-old amusement park has been adding coasters like they're going out of style (page 71).

◖ **Gettysburg National Military Park:** Site of the Civil War's most hellish battle, this national park is heaven for history buffs (page 110).

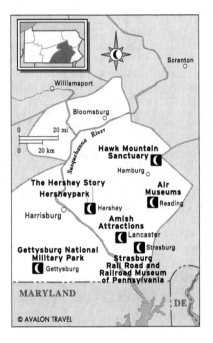

LOOK FOR ◖ TO FIND RECOMMENDED SIGHTS, ACTIVITIES, DINING, AND LODGING.

with musket-toting reenactors. The region is also home to the state capital, Harrisburg, and York County, the self-proclaimed "Factory Tour Capital of the World."

Travelers unfamiliar with the term Pennsylvania Dutch may wonder what south-central Pennsylvania has to do with the Netherlands. The answer is: nada. "Dutch," in this case, is generally regarded as a corruption of the word *Deutsch,* the German word for "German." Tens of thousands of German-speaking Europeans immigrated to Pennsylvania in the 18th century (before Germany as we know it existed). They, their descendants, and their English-influenced dialect came to be called Pennsylvania German, or Pennsylvania Dutch. A common misconception is that "Pennsylvania Dutch" is synonymous with "Amish." In fact, the Amish made up a very small percentage of the Germanic settlers. The overwhelming majority were affiliated with Lutheran or Reformed churches. But the Amish

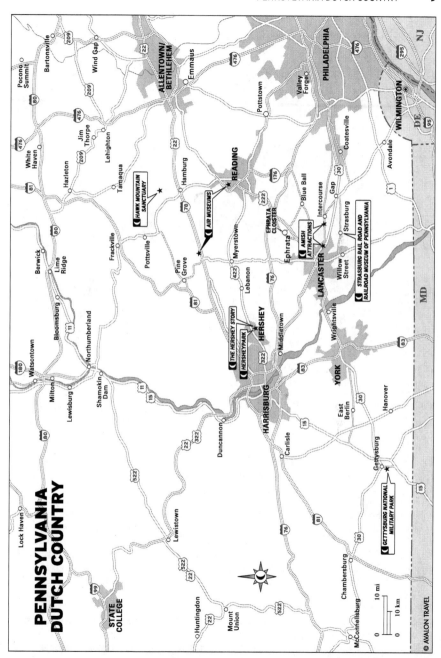

© WWW.DISCOVERLANCASTERPA.COM

laundry day in Lancaster County

and a handful of related "plain" groups have emerged as the guardians of the Pennsylvania Dutch dialect. They speak it at home and among friends. Amish children learn English as part of their formal education, which typically takes place in a one-room schoolhouse (think *Little House on the Prairie*) and ends after the eighth grade. *Wilkom* to Pennsylvania Dutch Country.

PLANNING YOUR TIME

You could spend weeks exploring the small, smaller, and smallest towns of Pennsylvania Dutch Country, but three or four days is sufficient time to hit the highlights. Plan to spend at least a day tootling around Lancaster County's Amish countryside, sharing the roads with horse-drawn buggies and buying direct from farmers and bakers, quilters and furniture makers. Keep in mind that the Amish and their "plain" cousins don't do business on Sundays. See to it that you eat at a restaurant serving Pennsylvania Dutch fare, preferably one that offers family-style dining. If your agenda also includes outlet shopping, save it for the evening. The Rockvale and Tanger outlets, just minutes apart along Lancaster County's main east–west thoroughfare, are open until 9 P.M. every day but Sunday,

when they close a few hours earlier. Anyone into antiques should plan to spend Sunday in Adamstown, a.k.a. "Antiques Capital USA," about 20 miles northeast of Lancaster city.

The Lancaster area is a good base of operations for exploring other parts of Pennsylvania Dutch Country. Reading is about 30 miles to Lancaster's northeast, Hershey and Harrisburg are 30–40 miles to its northwest, and Gettysburg is 55 miles to its southwest. There was a time when demand for rooms in Lancaster County far exceeded supply. Some visitors slept in their cars; others settled for hotels and motels as far as an hour away. The local chamber of commerce beseeched residents with spare rooms to open their doors to Amish-obsessed tourists, and many answered the call. Today the county boasts more than 150 B&Bs. Book a stay at a farm B&B to learn about Lancaster County's leading industry. (Tourism is a close second to agriculture.)

If you have kids, a visit to Hershey is nonnegotiable. You'll run yourself ragged trying to hit all the attractions in one day, so set aside two. A day is generally enough for Gettysburg, but ardent history buffs and ghost hunters can keep busy for several. York County's wineries and the Reading area's air museums are also worth a day trip.

Lancaster County

In January 1955, *Plain and Fancy* opened on Broadway. The musical comedy is the story of two New Yorkers who travel to Bird-in-Hand, Pennsylvania—a real-life village amid Lancaster County's Amish farmlands—to sell a piece of property they've inherited. There, just a few hours from home, they encounter a way of life completely foreign to them. The Amish, or "plain," lifestyle was completely foreign to most play-goers, too. A modest success on Broadway, the show sparked enormous interest in its setting. Before *Plain and Fancy*, Lancaster County was lucky to get 25,000 visitors a year. After, the number rocketed to more than two million. Tourists traipsed through farm fields, knocked on doors, and peered through windows in their quest for a close encounter of the Amish kind. Today there's no need to trespass. Lancaster County, which now welcomes upwards of 10 million visitors annually, is flush with information centers, attractions, and tour operators offering an Amish 101 curriculum.

About 250,000 Amish live in North America, according to the Young Center for Anabaptist and Pietist Studies at Lancaster County's Elizabethtown College. Though the church originated in Europe, it's extinct there. Lancaster County is home to about 30,000 Amish—roughly half of Pennsylvania's Amish—and is neck and neck with Ohio's Holmes County for the distinction of having the world's largest Amish settlement. It also holds the distinction of having the oldest surviving Amish settlement in the world. The first ship carrying a significant group of Amish from their homelands in central Europe to the New World docked in Philadelphia in 1737. Some of the Amish passengers made their home in Lancaster County; a larger number settled 20-odd miles away in present-day Berks County. While the Amish all but disappeared from Berks County by the early 1800s, Lancaster County had six congregations (known as church districts) at the close of

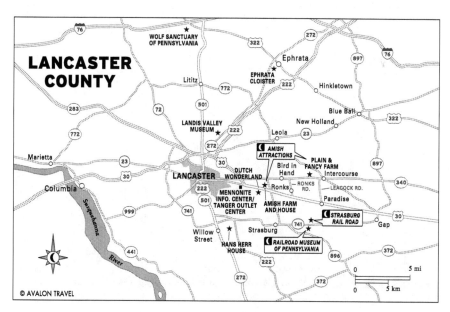

the century. Their numbers have soared since then, more than doubling between 1980 and 2000 and climbing more than 30 percent in the first decade of this century. Large families have a lot to do with the vigorous growth: Most Amish couples have five or more children. And while Amish teens are allowed a period of *rumspringa,* or "running around," during which they decide whether to join the church, very few leave the fold. Given the chance to drive cars and dress how they please, more than 85 percent ultimately choose the horse and buggy as their mode of transport and the distinctive garb that sets them apart from the "English;" i.e., everyone else.

As you explore the region, keep in mind that that not all traditionally dressed people are Amish. Some conservative Mennonite and Brethren groups also practice "plain" dress. You may not be able to tell them apart, but each has distinguishing characteristics.

There's more to Lancaster County than its Amish population. The county seat, Lancaster city, boasts a thriving arts scene. Rail fans will find an abundance of train-related attractions in and around the town of Strasburg. Antiques enthusiasts will fall in love with Adamstown, a.k.a. "Antiques Capital USA."

Bargain hunters can get their fix at a pair of outlet malls along U.S. 30. Anyone fascinated by the Amish and their strict codes of conduct will likely be fascinated by the towns of Lititz and Ephrata. The former began as an experiment in utopia by members of a Protestant denomination that prohibited everything from dancing to changing professions without approval from church elders. The latter was home to a religious group so disdainful of worldly pleasures that its members slept on wooden pillows. Other Lancaster County communities are remarkable for their names: Intercourse, Paradise, Blue Ball, Fertility, and, of course, Bird-in-Hand.

◖ AMISH ATTRACTIONS

If you're visiting Lancaster County for the number one reason people visit Lancaster County—to see the Amish—you may be at a loss as to where to start. Unlike malls and museums, amusement parks and ski resorts, the Amish are an attraction without an address. You can't punch "Amish" into your GPS and get turn-by-turn directions. They're people living their lives—people who don't necessarily appreciate being the focus of tourists' attention. And while it's not hard to catch sight of them

© ANNA DUBROVSKY

buggy ride

living their lives, you'll shortchange yourself if you don't garner some understanding of why they live the way they do.

Plain & Fancy Farm, the Amish Farm and House, and the Mennonite Information Center are great places to acquaint yourself with the ways of the Amish. Visiting one is quite enough. Each offers a hearty menu of get-to-know-the-Amish options. Choosing between the attractions is a matter of taste. Plain & Fancy is smack dab in the heart of Amish country, while the other two are located along U.S. 30, a major east–west thoroughfare. It's the only one that offers buggy rides through the countryside and the opportunity to visit an Amish family in their home. But it's also the priciest of the three. The Amish Farm and House is your best bet if you're traveling with kids. It's crawling with animals and offers a variety of children's activities, including pony rides, a corn maze, and "Buttercup," a life-sized fiberglass cow always ready to be milked. While all three offer driving tours of Amish farmlands, the Mennonite Information Center is unique in that it doesn't operate tour vans or buses. Instead, a guide will climb into your car and lead you on a personal tour. It's the way to go if you tend to ask a lot of questions. It's also a great value: just $44 for a vehicle carrying as many as seven people. On the downside, the Mennonite Information Center is closed on Sundays.

Plain & Fancy Farm

In 1958, a few years after *Plain and Fancy* hit the Broadway stage, a man named Walter Smith built an Amish-style house and barn along Route 340, midway between the villages of Bird-in-Hand and Intercourse, with the intent of giving house tours and holding barn dances. Shrewdly, he named the property after the Broadway musical that ignited so much interest in Amish country. Half a century later, Plain & Fancy Farm (3121 Old Philadelphia Pike, Bird-in-Hand, www.plain andfancyfarm.com) offers everything a tourist could ask for: food, lodging, souvenirs, and an excellent orientation to the Amish way of life.

(Alas, it doesn't offer dances. The barn Mr. Smith built opened as Lancaster County's first family-style restaurant in 1959.)

Begin your orientation to the Amish way of life at the **Amish Experience Theater** (717/768-3600, ext. 210, www.amish experience.com, show begins on the hour 9 A.M.–5 P.M. Mon.–Sat. and 11 A.M.–5 P.M. Sun. Apr.–Oct., 10 A.M.–5 P.M. Mon.–Sat. and 11 A.M.–5 P.M. Sun. Nov.–Dec., call or check website for winter hours, admission $9.95, children 4–12 $6.95). This is not your garden-variety movie theater. Designed to look like a barn, it features five screens, a fog machine, and other bells and whistles that produce three-dimensional effects. *Jacob's Choice,* the film for which the theater was built, packs some 400 years of history into 40 minutes. It's the contemporary story of an Old Order Amish family and the teenage son torn between joining the church and leaving the fold for a modern life. As the title character learns about the persecution Anabaptists faced in Europe and their journey to the New World, so does the audience. Consider yourself warned: The early history of Anabaptism is rated R for violence. Filmed locally in 1995, *Jacob's Choice* doesn't dwell on the blood and gore, but a burning-at-the-stake scene could rattle children.

Tickets for tours of the house Mr. Smith built back in 1958 are sold in the theater lobby. Now known as the **Amish Country Homestead** (717/768-3600, ext. 210, www .amishexperience.com, admission $9.95, children 4–12 $6.95), the nine-room house is continually updated to reflect changes in the Amish lifestyle. (Contrary to popular belief, the Amish don't live just as they did centuries ago. For one thing, they have refrigerators.) The schedule varies throughout the year, but during peak season—April through October—tours begin at 15 minutes before the hour 9:45 A.M.–3:45 P.M. Monday–Saturday and 10:45 A.M.–3:45 P.M. Sunday, with an additional tour at 4:15 P.M. daily. Guides explain such head-scratchers as why the Amish eschew electricity but use refrigerators and other appliances powered by propane gas. The tour takes about 40 minutes. A package rate for admission to *Jacob's Choice* and the house is available.

Driving tours of the farmlands that surround Plain & Fancy depart from the theater lobby. The two-hour **Amish Farmlands Tour** (717/768-3600, ext. 210, www.amishexperience.com, $29.95 per person, children 4–12 $14.95) is offered Saturdays in March, daily from late March through November, and weekends in December. Stops may include roadside produce stands, bakeries, a wine shop, and a working farm. Ask about the SuperSaver Package if you're interested in *Jacob's Choice,* the house tour, and the Farmlands Tour. Offered weekday evenings from mid-June through October, the **V.I.P. Tour** ($45.95 per person) is a pricey but priceless experience. You don't have to be a "very important person" to sign up for the three-hour excursion. V.I.P., in this case, stands for "Visit in Person." The tour visits an Amish dairy farm during milking time, proceeds to a meeting with an Amish quilter, furniture maker, basket weaver, or other craftsperson, and culminates in a sit-down chat with an Amish family in their home. V.I.P. Tours are limited to 14 people and normally sell out, so you'll want to purchase tickets in advance.

No reservation needed to hit the back roads in a horse-drawn buggy or wagon. **Aaron and Jessica's Buggy Rides** (9 A.M.–dusk Mon.–Sat. and 10 A.M.–5 P.M. Sun. Apr.–Nov., 9 A.M.–4:30 P.M. Mon.–Sat. Dec.–Mar., 717/768-8828, www.amishbuggyrides.com) depart from Plain & Fancy Farm every 10 minutes or so. Trips range from 20 minutes to over an hour, with prices starting at $10 for adults and $6 for children 3–12. Children 2 and under ride for free. Aaron and Jessica's—named for owner Jack Meyer's oldest daughter and her first horse—bills itself as the county's only buggy tour operator staffed entirely by "plain" people (except on Sundays, which they set aside for worship).

Spending the night at Plain & Fancy Farm is as easy as booking a stay at the amenity-rich **AmishView Inn & Suites** (866/735-1600, www.amishviewinn.com, room $114–214,

Jack Meyer, owner of Aaron and Jessica's Buggy Rides

suite $174–424). Ask for a room on the backside of the hotel, where you'll enjoy gorgeous vistas of Amish farms.

The Amish Farm and House

The easiest way to find the Amish Farm and House (2395 Lincoln Hwy. East, Lancaster, 717/394-6185, www.amishfarmandhouse.com, 10 A.M.–4 P.M. daily Jan.–Mar., 9 A.M.–5 P.M. Apr.–May, 8:30 A.M.–6 P.M. June–Aug., 9 A.M.–5 P.M. Sept.–Oct., 9 A.M.–4 P.M. Nov.–Dec., general admission $8.25, seniors $7.50, children 5–11 $5.25) is to look for its neighbor, a Target. The bullseye logo of the discount store, which opened in 2005 on property carved from the hundreds-year-old farm, is far easier to spot than the 70-foot windmill or barn and silo that once dominated the skyline. Their juxtaposition is emblematic of the Amish community's insoluble dilemma: modernity.

Opened to the public in July 1955, the Amish Farm and House bills itself as the first tourist attraction in Lancaster County and the first Amish attraction in the United States. The operating farm has since shrunk from 25 acres to 15 (making room for Target, PetSmart, Panera, etc.), but there's more to see than ever. Start with a guided tour of the farmhouse, included in general admission. Built in 1805 of limestone quarried on the property, the house has counted Quakers, Mennonites, and Amish as residents. Today it's furnished in the manner of a typical Amish home. The front room features wooden benches arranged in preparation for a church service, opening the door for a discussion of why the Amish worship in their homes and other aspects of their religion. Their manner of dress is explained in the bedrooms. After the 45-minute tour, explore the farm at your own pace. Children love the chicken house, the 1803 stone bank barn with its cows, horses, and pigs, and the outdoor animal pens. A goat playground makes for a great photo op with the frisky ruminants. Kids (we're talking humans now, not goats) also enjoy the corn maze, up and running mid-July through October, and tootling around on Amish scooters when weather permits. Other farm features

amid malls, the Amish Farm and House

© ANNA DUBROVSKY

the goat playground at the Amish Farm and House

include an original tobacco shed, one of the few remaining lime kilns in Lancaster County, a working waterwheel, a circa 1855 covered bridge, and a one-room Amish schoolhouse built specifically for tourists in 2006. A quilter and woodcarver are on-site April through October, demonstrating their skills and selling their works. You'll catch a blacksmith pounding away in the Civil War–era blacksmith shop during special events such as **Sheep Shearing Days** (late Apr./early May). Short **buggy rides** ($5 per person) around the property are offered in June, July, and August.

A 90-minute **bus tour of the countryside** (adults $18.95, children 5–11 $12.95, children 4 and under $4.95) leaves from the Amish Farm and House multiple times a day year-round. Call or check the website for a schedule of tour times. It's a good idea to make a reservation, especially if visiting April through October. The tour includes a stop at at least one Amish business (except on Sundays, when the Amish don't conduct business). The package rate for touring the house, farm, and countryside is $25.95

for adults, $15.95 for children 5–11, and $4.95 for children 4 and under. The Amish Farm and House also offers bus tours of downtown Lancaster (April–Oct.) and the region's covered bridges (mid-June–Oct.).

Mennonite Information Center

Don't be put off by its name. You *will* learn about the Amish at the Mennonite Information Center (2209 Millstream Rd., Lancaster, 717/299-0954, www.mennoniteinfoctr.com, 8 A.M.–5 P.M. Mon.–Sat. Apr.–Oct., 8:30 A.M.–4:30 P.M. Mon.–Sat. Nov.–March), located next to Tanger Outlet Center. Start by watching the three-screen feature *"Who Are the Amish?"* (on the hour 9 A.M.–4 P.M., admission $5, seniors $4.50, children 7–12 $3). It answers such questions as: How many are there? Why do they dress that way? Why do they drive buggies? And what do they have against electricity? The images are beautiful and the narration intelligent, but at 30 minutes long, the movie won't necessarily hold the attention of young children. Also showing: the 17-minute *Postcards from a Heritage of Faith,* which elucidates the similarities and differences between the Amish and Mennonites, both of which trace their roots to the Anabaptist movement in 16th-century Europe. There's no charge to see the shorter film, shown on the half hour from 8:30 A.M. to 4:30 P.M. except from November through March, when the last showing is at 3:30 P.M. Admission to the information center's exhibits on Anabaptist life is also free.

Movies and exhibits are nice, but what sets the Mennonite Information Center apart are its **personal tours of Amish country.** For less than the cost of two seats on many bus tours, a guide will hop in your vehicle and point the way to Amish farms, one-room schoolhouses, quilt shops, covered bridges, etc. All guides have a Mennonite or Amish heritage and have lived in Lancaster County for most, if not all, of their lives. A two-hour tour for a carful of up to seven people is $44. Each additional hour is $14. Call ahead to arrange for a guide to meet you at a specified time or just show up and request a tour. The wait for a guide is rarely longer than 30 minutes. Another great service from the Mennonite Information Center is its list of **Mennonite guest homes,** available on its website or in pamphlet form at the info center.

The information center is home to a life-sized reproduction of the portable place of worship described in the Biblical account of the Israelites' exodus from ancient Egypt. A wax figure of the high priest sports a breastplate of gold and precious stones. The **Biblical Tabernacle Reproduction** (admission $7, seniors $6, children 7–12 $4) can only be seen by guided tour. Tours begin on the hour 9 A.M.–4 P.M. from April through October and 10 A.M.–3 P.M. in March and November. From December through February they're offered at 10 A.M., noon, and 2 P.M. A package rate for admission to *"Who Are the Amish?"* and the tabernacle reproduction is available. The reproduction has no real connection to Lancaster County's Anabaptist communities. It was constructed in the 1940s by a Baptist minister in St. Petersburg, Florida, purchased by Mennonites in the 1950s, and installed in

its current home in the 1970s. The information center sells a variety of tabernacle model kits, fair-trade handicrafts from around the world, and a wide selection of books about Anabaptist history and faith.

Next door to the info center is the headquarters of the **Lancaster Mennonite Historical Society** (2215 Millstream Rd., 717/393-9745, www.lmhs.org, 8:30 A.M.–4:30 P.M. Tues.–Sat.), which also boasts a fantastic bookstore. It's home to a museum (admission $5, seniors $4.50, children 7–12 $3) showcasing Pennsylvania German artifacts, a 30,000-book library, and the largest Mennonite archives in the eastern United States and Canada.

DOWNTOWN LANCASTER
It's not unusual for tourists to come and go from Lancaster County without so much as stepping foot in downtown Lancaster. Many are entirely unaware that the county has an urban center. It's hard to blame them. Lancaster County's countryside and quaint towns have gotten all the press for decades. It doesn't help that its major east-west thoroughfare, U.S. 30, bypasses downtown Lancaster altogether. Well, downtown's museums and merchants have had just about enough of being ignored. Revitalization efforts in recent years have given downtown a fresh look and its boosters more cred. Now, in addition to boasting the oldest continuously operated farmers market, theater, and tobacco shop in the U.S., downtown boasts a new convention center and adjoining 19-floor hotel. New restaurants, stores, and galleries add to its promotional arsenal. Plan on devoting a day to downtown. Make it a Tuesday, Friday, or Saturday, when the farmers market is open. Ideally, make it the first Friday of any month, when museums, galleries, and shops stay open as late as 9 P.M. **First Fridays** (717/509-2787, www.lancasterarts.com) feature special exhibitions, artists receptions, and live entertainment.

Guided Tours
The city of Lancaster is so steeped in history—it was capital of the 13 colonies for one day during the American Revolution and capital

of Pennsylvania for 13 years—that a guided tour is a good idea. You can choose your mode: walking, gliding, or riding.

Led by a volunteer guide in 18th- or 19th-century garb, the **Historic Lancaster Walking Tour** (Lancaster Visitors Center, 5 W. King St., 717/392-1776, www.historiclancaster walkingtour.com, $7 per person, seniors $6, children $1) visits more than 50 sites. Allow about 90 minutes for the tour, which begins with a DVD presentation. It's offered daily April–October. On Tuesdays, Fridays, and Saturdays, when nearby Central Market is open, tours depart at 10 A.M. and 1 P.M. Only a 1 P.M. tour is offered on other days.

If you prefer gliding to walking, head over to **Red Rose Seg Tours** (305 N. Queen St., 717/393-4526, www.redrosesegtours.com, guided tour $55–65 per person, mini-glide $25). Opened in 2009 by a local couple that became enamored of Segway tours during their travels, Red Rose offers general tours of downtown as well as arts- and ghost-themed tours. You don't need gliding experience, but you do need a valid driver's license. Each hour-long tour is preceded by 20–30 minutes of training and practice. The tours are offered Wednesday–Sunday from March through December. Call or visit the website for departure times. Tours are available by appointment in January and February. Want the Segway experience but not the tour? Schedule a "mini-glide."

The **Amish Farm and House** (2395 Lincoln Hwy. East, 717/394-6185, www.amishfarm andhouse.com), located on U.S. 30 several miles east of downtown Lancaster, offers a two-hour bus tour of the city. Departing at 10 A.M. on Tuesdays, Fridays, and Saturdays from April through October, the tour is $29.95 for adults, $19.95 for children 5–11, and $4.95 for younger children.

Central Market

Central Market (23 N. Market St., 717/735-6890, www.centralmarketlancaster.com, 6 A.M.–4 P.M. Tues. and Fri., 6 A.M.–2 P.M. Sat.) is the pulsing heart of the city. Granted, the indoor farmers market pulses just three days

© ANNA DUBROVSKY

Central Market in downtown Lancaster

a week, but given its advanced age, it's incredible that it pulses at all. Central Market is the oldest continually operated farmers market in the country. When Lancaster was laid out in the 1730s, a lot adjacent to the town square was designated as a public marketplace in perpetuity. In its early years, the market was simply an open space where farmers and others could sell their wares. The current market house, an eye-catching Romanesque Revival structure with two towers and ornate brick and stone work, was built in 1889. Many of the 60-some market stands have been operated by multiple generations of the same family. The Stoner's vegetable stand, famous for its arugula, has been around for more than a century. Fresh produce isn't the half of it. Central Market is one-stop shopping for everything from hand-stitched Amish quilts to foie gras. There's beef, poultry, and fish; milk and cheeses; breads and pastries; coffees and teas; candies and candles; preserves and prepared foods. There's even a stand specializing in horseradish products. Beware the fan that circulates the scent of fresh grated horseradish. Come on the early side for the best selection. On Tuesdays and Fridays, many of the vendors call it quits at 3 P.M., an hour before the market closes.

Heritage Center Museum

A stone's throw from Central Market is a building that once served as Lancaster's city hall and even as Pennsylvania's capitol. (Lancaster had a 13-year run as the state capital, ceding the role to Harrisburg in 1812.) Today it's one of two 1790s buildings constituting the Heritage Center Museum (5 W. King St., 717/299-6440, www.lancasterheritage.com, 9 A.M.–5 P.M. Mon.–Sat., 10 A.M.–3 P.M. Sun., open until 9 P.M. First Fridays, free admission), which houses an extensive collection of 18th- to 20th-century decorative arts indigenous to south-central Pennsylvania. The stories of groups who settled in the region, including the Amish, Mennonites, Quakers, and Moravians, are told through their furniture, folk art, and other works. The exhibits are worth a look, especially because admission is free, but the museum's best feature is its store. It's chock-full of jewelry, pottery, carvings, clocks, glassware, and other creations by area artisans. If the size doesn't fit or the color doesn't suit, don't lose heart. Many of the artisans are happy to customize pieces.

Lancaster Quilt & Textile Museum *CLOSED*

The Heritage Center's sister museum, the Lancaster Quilt & Textile Museum (37 Market St., 717/397-2970, www.quiltandtextilemuseum.com, 10 A.M.–5 P.M. Mon. and Wed.–Thurs., 9 A.M.–5 P.M. Tues. and Fri.–Sat., open until 9 P.M. First Fridays, admission $6, students $4, children 17 and under free, no charge after 5 P.M. on First Fridays), is also a few paces from Central Market. The museum was conceived in 2002, when the Heritage Center got its hands on a blockbuster collection of 19th- and 20th-century Amish quilts known as the Esprit Collection. Started by Esprit Corp. founder Doug Tompkins, it's regarded by many scholars as the finest collection of its kind. The Heritage Center, which had its own hoard of quilts and textiles made in

If you catch the quilting bug at the Lancaster Quilt & Textile Museum, pick up a quilt kit at the museum store.

© WWW.DISCOVERLANCASTERPA.COM

The Lancaster Quilt & Textile Museum is home to the famed Esprit Collection.

south-central Pennsylvania, then got its hands on a grand Beaux Arts building. Originally owned by a community bank that didn't survive the Great Depression, the 1912 building had stood empty for much of its life. It opened as the Quilt & Textile Museum in 2004. The marriage of cosmopolitan architecture and folk art works. If you catch the quilting bug, pop into the museum store for a do-it-yourself kit. The store also sells Amish-made quilts, including Esprit Collection reproductions, and unique items such as framed miniature quilts.

Art Museums and Galleries

Art lovers can fill a day exploring Lancaster's museums and galleries. There are more than a dozen within a few blocks of Penn Square (intersection of King and Queen Streets). The section of Prince Street between King Street and Walnut Street to its north is especially crowded with galleries. Very definitely worth a stop: the **Red Raven Art Company** (138 N. Prince St., 717/299-4400, www.redravenartcompany.com, 10 A.M.–5 P.M. Tues. and Thurs.–Sat., open

until 8:30 P.M. First Fridays), which showcases the works of a band of fine artists from the area. Red Raven sets aside space for fledgling artists—art students even—and doesn't take a commission on their sales. If you lean more toward folk art than fine art, you'll love **CityFolk** (146 N. Prince St., 717/393-8807, www.lancasterarts .com, 10 A.M.–5 P.M. Mon.–Sat., winter hours 10 A.M.–4 P.M. Tues.–Sat., open until 9 P.M. First Fridays) with its ever-changing galleries of furniture, paintings, carvings, pottery, and other works by artists and craftspeople from around the country. CityFolk also offers antiques and garden art. A handy map of the city's arts and cultural venues is available on the website of the nonprofit LancasterARTS (717/509-2787, www .lancasterarts.com), their tireless promoter.

A short walk east of Penn Square is the one-time home of Lancaster's most acclaimed artist, the modernist painter Charles Demuth. It's now open to the public as the **Demuth Museum** (120 E. King St., 717/299-9940, www.demuth.org, 10 A.M.–4 P.M. Tues.–Sat., 1–4 P.M. Sun., closed Jan., free admission).

Demuth was born in Lancaster in 1883 and died there in 1935 but moved in avant-garde circles in places as far-flung as Paris, New York, and Bermuda. He was very much appreciated during his lifetime, earning a place in the permanent collection of New York's Metropolitan Museum of Art by his 40s. Among his best-known works is the Precisionist masterpiece *My Egypt,* inspired by grain elevators in Lancaster and snapped up by the Whitney Museum in New York. Demuth's eponymous museum boasts 40 works from throughout his career, plus an extensive archive and library. One of its main galleries is the artist's former studio, a second-floor room overlooking a garden that was tended by his mother. A fertile source of inspiration for his floral watercolors, the garden is open to museum visitors. Rotating exhibits showcase works by Demuth's contemporaries or artists with a thematic or stylistic connection to him. Next door to the museum is the **Demuth Tobacco Shop** (114 E. King St., 717/397-6613, www.demuthtobaccoshop .com, 9 A.M.–5 P.M. Mon.–Fri., 9 A.M.–3 P.M. Sat.), which was owned by the Demuth family for more than two centuries. Established in 1770, it's said to be the oldest tobacco shop in the country.

Not to be forgotten is the **Lancaster Museum of Art** (135 N. Lime St., 717/394-3497, www.lmapa.org, 10 A.M.–4 P.M. Tues.–Sat., noon–4 P.M. Sun., open until 8 P.M. First Fridays, free admission), home to an extensive collection of works by contemporary regional artists. Perhaps more striking than any piece in the collection is the museum's home: a remarkably intact example of Greek Revival–style domestic architecture. The Grubb Mansion, as it's called, was built in the 1840s for an iron master with an eye for art.

Lancaster Science Factory

Geared for children 7–13, the Science Factory (454 New Holland Ave., 717/509-6363, www .lancastersciencefactory.org, 10 A.M.–5 P.M. Mon.–Sat. and noon–5 P.M. Sun., closed Mon. Sept.–May, admission $7.50, seniors $6.50, children 3–15 $6) features dozens of interactive exhibits that help visitors—even those well over 13—understand such things as electricity, magnetism, acoustics, and fluid dynamics. If your kids like blowing bubbles, they'll love the "minimal surfaces" exhibit. Budding Beethovens can experiment with the "bongophone," a bongo/xylophone. The Fac, which opened in 2008 after five years in the making, isn't the only science museum in Lancaster. Less than two miles away is the **North Museum of Natural History & Science** (400 College Ave., 717/291-3941, www.northmuseum.org, 10 A.M.–5 P.M. Tues.–Sat., noon–5 P.M. Sun., museum admission $7, seniors and children 3–17 $6, museum and planetarium admission $8.50, seniors and children $7.50), which boasts a dinosaur gallery, a live animal room, and a planetarium. Located on the campus of Franklin & Marshall College since the 1950s, the museum plans to build a new facility nearby.

"TRAIN TOWN USA"

The town of **Strasburg,** some nine miles southwest of downtown Lancaster, bills itself as "the real Lancaster County." Which is to

Strasburg Rail Road

say that it has changed little in the last couple of centuries. Buggies clip-clop through the town square at the intersection of Routes 741 and 896. Families stream in and out of the old-timey **Strasburg Country Store & Creamery** (1 W. Main St., Strasburg, 717/687-0766, www.strasburg.com, 11 A.M.–10 P.M. Mon.–Sat., noon–10 P.M. Sun.), where scoops of homemade ice cream are pressed into just-made waffle cones. Much of *Witness,* the 1985 romantic thriller that did more for tourism to Amish country than any marketing campaign, was filmed on a farm nearby.

But what brings tourists here by the busload is train mania. There are half a dozen train-related attractions within two miles of the square, including the **Red Caboose Motel & Restaurant** (312 Paradise Ln., Ronks, 717/687-5000, www.redcaboosemotel.com, lodging $69–159, dining $4–17), where rail fans bed down and chow down in refurbished train cars. The Strasburg area is such a magnet for "foamers," as the most zealous of rail fans are known, that it's sometimes called "Train Town USA" (not to be confused with "Railroad

City," a.k.a. Altoona, three hours away). The oldest of the attractions and a good place to start is the Strasburg Rail Road. Don't leave town without a visit to the Choo Choo Barn, where you can see the historic railroad and much more in miniature.

From the town square, head east on Route 741 (Main Street). You'll see the Choo Choo Barn and Strasburg Train Shop on your right after half a mile. Half a mile later, you'll arrive at the Strasburg Rail Road and Railroad Museum of Pennsylvania, located on opposite sides of Route 741. Continue to the next intersection and turn left onto Paradise Lane to check into the Red Caboose or check out the National Toy Train Museum.

◖ Strasburg Rail Road and the Railroad Museum of Pennsylvania

Incorporated in 1832, the Strasburg Rail Road (300 Gap Rd., Ronks, 717/687-7522, www .strasburgrailroad.com, regular train ticket $14–25, children 3–11 $7–25, toddlers free–$25) is America's oldest operating short-line

Railroad Museum of Pennsylvania

railroad. It was almost abandoned in the late 1950s, after an upsurge in the use of highways for freight transportation and a series of storms that destroyed parts of its 4.5-mile track. But rail fans came to its rescue, turning it into a tourist attraction and a time capsule of early-20th-century railroading. The railroad offers trips to Paradise and back—as in Paradise, PA—every month but January. As its painstakingly restored trains steam past fields still plowed by horses and mules, conductors share tidbits about the railroad's history and the Amish lifestyle. Horse-drawn buggies wait at railroad crossings. In the hopes that future generations of riders are treated to the same tranquil scenery, a nickel of every ticket sold goes toward farmland preservation. Ticket prices vary widely depending on the type of passenger car. A ride in an open-air car, for example, is $16 for adults, $9 for children 3–11, and $2 for tots, while seats in the plush President's Car, once used by the top brass of the Reading Railroad, are $25 regardless of age. Combo tickets good for a train ride and admission to the nearby Railroad Museum of Pennsylvania are available. In addition to regular rides, which depart as frequently as every half hour on operating days, the Strasburg Rail Road offers a variety of themed excursions. It's a good idea to purchase tickets in advance for the Wine & Cheese Train ($35), murder mystery dinners ($59.95, children 5–11 $39.95), Santa's Paradise Express ($17–25, children 3–11 $10–25, toddlers $3–25), and other special trips. For several days each June, September, and November, fans of Thomas the Tank Engine can ride behind a full-sized steam locomotive based on the storybook character. **Day Out With Thomas** tickets are $18 for passengers 2 and older.

The nine-mile round-trip takes just 45 minutes, but if you're into trains or traveling with kids, plan to spend a couple of hours or longer at the home station. A guided tour of the railroad's mechanical shop ($16 with train ticket stub, $25 without) is offered at noon on most operating days. The 50-minute tour is limited to 25 people and often sells out. Rail fans will also want to visit an 1885 switch tower

© WWW.DISCOVERLANCASTERPA.COM

Thomas the Tank Engine chugs into Strasburg Rail Road each June, September, and November.

(suggested donation $2) that affords a bird's-eye view of approaching trains. Kids can operate a vintage pump car or take a ride in a circa 1920 miniature steam train. Wee ones can pilot hand-propelled "cranky cars" dating to the 1930s. The station also features several stores geared toward train lovers, a café, and a sweets shop. Consider packing a picnic basket or buying a boxed lunch at the station and disembarking the train at Groff's Grove, a picnic area near Cherry Crest Adventure Farm and its Amazing Maize Maze. (The Strasburg Rail Road sells discounted Cherry Crest tickets.) Just don't miss the last train back.

Directly across the street from the Strasburg Rail Road, the Railroad Museum of Pennsylvania (300 Gap Rd., Ronks, 717/687-8628, www.rrmuseumpa.org, 9 A.M.–5 P.M. Mon.–Sat. and noon–5 P.M. Sun., closed Mon. Nov.–Mar., admission $10, seniors $9, children 3–11 $8) boasts a world-class collection of railroad artifacts, including many last-of-their-kind locomotives. More than 50 locomotives and railroad cars are housed in its 100,000-square-foot exhibit hall. Dozens of others reside in the restoration yard, which is open to visitors when weather and staffing permit. Behind-the-scenes tours of the restoration shop, normally closed to the public for safety reasons, are offered at noon and 4 P.M. most days. The fee is $10 per person and directly benefits the restoration program.

Rail fans hoping to find a rare "Big Boy" steam locomotive will be disappointed. The museum, which opened in 1975, is owned and operated by the Pennsylvania Historical and Museum Commission and endeavors to preserve objects relating to the history of railroading in Pennsylvania. The legendary Big Boys didn't ply Pennsylvania's rails. With its 195-ton engine, Pennsylvania Railroad "Mountain" No. 6755 is the largest and heaviest steam locomotive in the museum's collection. Another highlight of the collection: Pennsylvania Railroad E6 No. 460, a steam locomotive dubbed the "Lindbergh Engine." After Charles Lindbergh completed the first nonstop solo flight across the Atlantic in 1927, the aviator was summoned to Washington, D.C., for a fete in his honor. Fiercely competitive news organizations hired airplanes to fly films of the event to New York; one engaged the Pennsylvania Railroad. No. 460 made the run in record time, and the film it carried was the first to arrive in theaters. Word spread that the locomotive had outraced airplanes. (In reality, credit goes to the maverick news organization, which managed to process, edit, and copy its film en route. But it certainly helped that No. 460 traveled at speeds of up to 115 miles per hour.)

National Toy Train Museum

Real trains are well and good, but there's something enchanting about their much-shrunken kin. Which makes the National Toy Train Museum (300 Paradise Ln., Strasburg, 717/687-8976, www.nttmuseum.org, 10 A.M.–5 P.M. Fri.–Mon. May–Oct., 10 A.M.–5 P.M. Sat.–Sun. in Apr. and Nov.–Dec., admission $6, seniors $5, children 6–12 $3, family $15) an exceptionally enchanting place. It houses one of the most extensive collections of toy trains in the world. More than 100 different manufacturers are represented in the museum's collection, which includes some of the earliest and rarest toy trains. It also includes some model trains. (What's the difference? Toy trains are generally marketed to youngsters and not necessarily based on real trains. Model trains aspire to look

the National Toy Train Museum

© ANNA DUBROVSKY

every bit like real trains.) The museum, which aspires to look like a Victorian-era station, has five large train layouts. Each has trains of a different scale and represents a different period of the 20th century. Visitors have the opportunity to operate many choo-choos themselves.

The museum is operated by the Train Collectors Association, which has its national headquarters there. Those new to "the world's greatest hobby," as the TCA calls it, can learn the ropes via video presentations in the museum. Seasoned collectors can bury their noses in repair guides, trade catalogs, and other materials in the reference library. While the museum is closed January–March, the library is open five days a week year-round. Call for hours.

Choo Choo Barn

Model train enthusiasts can also find nirvana at the Choo Choo Barn (226 Gap Rd., Strasburg, 717/687-7911, www.choochoobarn .com, 10 A.M.–5 P.M. daily mid-Mar.–Dec., admission $6, children 4–12 $3.25), which predates the National Toy Train Museum. The family-owned attraction has just one layout: a massive, marvelous display featuring 22 trains and more than 150 animated figures and vehicles. Local landmarks including the Strasburg Rail Road and Dutch Wonderland amusement park are represented. There's an Amish barn-raising and an operating quarry, a zoo and a three-ring circus, a baseball game and a ski slope. There's even a fire scene, complete with flames.

The Choo Choo Barn traces its history to 1945, when Strasburg native George Groff, recently returned from war, gave his toddler son a Lionel train set for Christmas. With each year, the train display in their basement grew bigger and more elaborate. They began opening it to townspeople and local school groups at Christmastime. In 1961 the Groffs moved their now 600-square-foot layout to a barn-like building just west of the recently reopened Strasburg Rail Road. The Choo Choo Barn proved a hit, and the display has since grown to more than 1,700 square feet. The family

business has grown to include several specialty shops next to the Barn. The **Strasburg Train Shop** (717/687-0464, www.etrainshop.com), which caters to the layout builder, is known as the place to go for uncommon things such as garbage cans. **Thomas' Trackside Station** (717/687-7911, www.ttstation.com) carries more than 1,200 items related to the *Thomas and Friends* children's television series and the distinction of being the only all-Thomas store in the country. The Groffs also opened a shop specializing in railroading books and videos. The shops are open 10 A.M.–5 P.M. daily.

OTHER SIGHTS
President James Buchanan's Wheatland

The only U.S. president from Pennsylvania lived—and died—on a handsome estate west of downtown Lancaster. James Buchanan, also remembered as the only bachelor to lead the nation, was secretary of state when he moved to Wheatland (230 N. President Ave., Lancaster, 717/392-4633, www.lancasterhistory.org, tours on the hour 10 A.M.–3 P.M. Tues.–Oct., 10 A.M.–3 P.M. Fri.–Sat. Nov.–Dec., weekdays by appointment Jan.–Mar., call or check website for special Christmas week hours, admission $8, seniors $7, students 12 and older $6, children 6–11 $3) in 1848. He announced his 1856 presidential campaign on the front porch of the Federal-style mansion. Reviled for his wishy-washiness on the subject of slavery and his handling of the secession crisis, the 15th president penned a defensive memoir after retiring to Wheatland in 1861. His writing desk is among the many artifacts displayed throughout the manse today. The collection includes everything from his White House china to his bathing tub and even a bottle of 1827 Madeira, now half evaporated, from his wine cellar. Tours leave from the visitors center behind the mansion, where exhibits and a short film introduce the man who reportedly had these words for his successor, Abraham Lincoln, on inauguration day in 1861: "If you are as happy in entering the White House as I shall feel on returning to Wheatland, you are

© ANNA DUBROVSKY

President James Buchanan's Wheatland

a happy man indeed." Buchanan died at his beloved Wheatland in 1868 and is buried at Woodward Hill Cemetery in Lancaster.

Wheatland shares its grounds and parking lot with **Lancaster County's Historical Society** (9:30 A.M.–9:30 P.M. Tues. and Thurs., 9:30 A.M.–4:30 P.M. Wed. and Fri.–Sat.), offering free changing exhibitions on local history.

Dutch Wonderland

Dutch Wonderland (2249 Lincoln Hwy. E., Lancaster, 717/291-1888, www.dutchwonder land.com) doesn't boast of adrenaline-pumping rides like many amusement parks. Its coaster count has stood at two for more than a decade, and you wouldn't call them hair-raising. "Kid-friendly" is what the park calls them. Founded in 1963 by a potato farmer with no experience in the amusement park industry, Dutch Wonderland is kid-friendly through and through. The 48-acre park, fronted by a castle facade visible from U.S. 30, bills itself as "A Kingdom for Kids." In addition to 30-some rides, none of which have a minimum height

requirement of more than 42 inches, Dutch Wonderland offers a variety of live shows daily. They're all quite delightful but none so much as the high-dive shows at Herr's Aqua Stadium. Performers twist, somersault, and splash their way through Disneyesque storylines. Duke's Dance Party, an interactive show hosted by a purple dragon with more than a passing resemblance to Barney, is also worth attending. Bring swimsuits for Duke's Lagoon, the park's water play area.

Dutch Wonderland is open weekends in May, daily from late May through Labor Day, and a few weekends after Labor Day. Gates open at 10 A.M. and close between 6 P.M. and 8:30 P.M. A variety of admission plans are available. One-day admission is $31.95 for guests ages 3–59, $26.95 for adults 60–69, $19.95 for those 70 and older. Hang on to your ticket stub in case you decide to come back the next day; consecutive-day admission is $25.95. Arrive within three hours of closing for twilight rates: $23.95 for guests ages 3–59, $22.95 for those 60 and older. A two-day flex pass, good for visits on any two days during the season, is $46.95 for anyone 3 or older. If your summer plans also include a visit to Hersheypark in nearby Hershey, ask about combo tickets. Hershey Entertainment & Resorts acquired Dutch Wonderland in 2001.

The park reopens in October for several weekends' worth of Halloween-themed fun and again during the holiday season, when it's draped in twinkling lights and visited by Santa.

Cherry Crest Adventure Farm

Dutch Wonderland isn't the only must-stop attraction for pint-sized visitors to Lancaster County. There's also Cherry Crest Adventure Farm (150 Cherry Hill Rd., Ronks, 717/687-6843 www.cherrycrestfarm.com), where every summer a five-acre cornfield is transformed into the Amazing Maize Maze. This maze is no cakewalk. It takes most visitors about an hour to find the exit. But there's no danger of getting hopelessly lost—or bored for that matter. Helpful "Maze Masters" are always on hand, and the paths are peppered with clues and diversions. There's even a Corn Café for mid-adventure refreshment. The maze, open from July 4 though early November, isn't the only attraction on the working farm. You can crawl through a hay tunnel, slide down a hay chute on a burlap sack, or hurl pumpkins with huge slingshots. You can ride pedal karts or a tractor-pulled wagon. You can even watch chicks hatch and hold the little fuzzballs. Now that's agritainment.

Cherry Crest is open Tuesday–Saturday from July 4 to Labor Day; Friday–Saturday and select other dates in September; and Thursday–Saturday from October until it closes in November. Hours vary. Admission to the maze and more than 30 other attractions is $14.95 for visitors 12 and older, $12.95 for kids 3–11. If you want to pass on the maze, admission is $11.95. Cherry Crest is also open on Saturdays and select other dates from Memorial Day weekend through June, offering a limited number of attractions for $8.95. There's an additional fee for the Make-a-Friend Workshop

(717/768-0152, www.makeafriendworkshop.com), available May–November. Kids can create a doll dressed in Amish-style garb or build a wooden barn, steam train, or tractor and wagon. The doll clothes and wooden pieces are Amish-made. Cherry Crest, which is not an Amish farm, is just east of Strasburg, less than three miles from the Strasburg Rail Road. In fact, the railroad's excursion trains run right through it. A "Railroad Farm Fun Pass," good for same-day adventuring at both attractions, is available.

Kitchen Kettle Village

Pat Burnley had two kids under 5 and was in the hospital about to give birth to a third when her husband, Bob, arrived with unexpected news: "We bought a business!" he told her. The business assets consisted of gas burners, a stack of two-gallon kettles, and a few jelly recipes. They set up shop in their garage. As word spread of the jelly "kitchen" in the Lancaster County town of Intercourse, more

Kitchen Kettle Village

the Jam & Relish Kitchen at Kitchen Kettle Village

© ANNA DUBROVSKY

and more people stopped to watch the process and have a taste. The business has come a long way from its humble beginnings in 1954. What used to be the family homestead is now Kitchen Kettle Village (3529 Old Philadelphia Pike, Intercourse, 717/768-8261, www.kitchen kettle.com, 9 A.M.–6 P.M. Mon.–Sat. May–Oct., 9 A.M.–5 P.M. Nov.–Apr.), home to about 40 specialty shops, a pair of restaurants, and a handful of kid-centric attractions. To call it a mall would fail to convey its quaintness. Think of it as a mall in a fairy tale—the sort of place where Snow White would buy ribbons for her hair. The canning kitchen is still the heart of it all. Its repertoire has grown to include not just jellies, jams, and preserves but also relishes, pickles, mustards, salad dressings, grilling sauces, and salsas—more than 80 products in all. The operation long outgrew the garage, but some things haven't changed: All products are made by hand in small batches, and visitors get a front-seat view. (Because the kitchen is staffed by Amish women, photos aren't permitted.) Plenty of visitors have discovered a taste for pickled beets or pepper jam in the store section of the **Jam & Relish Kitchen,** which abounds with samples. An attached bakery fills the air with the smells of shoofly pie, whoopie pies, molasses snaps, snickerdoodle cookies, and other local favorites.

Many of the village's shops feature locally made foods or goods, including ice cream from a dairy farm just a few miles away, fudge and kettle corn made on-site, hand-loomed clothing, fabric bags, quilts, and pottery. The house Pat Burnley (née Kling) grew up in is now the **Kling House Restaurant** (8 A.M.–3 P.M. Mon.–Thurs., 8 A.M.–4 P.M. Fri.–Sat., breakfast $4–9, lunch $8–15), which serves the likes of cinnamon-raisin French toast and baked oatmeal for breakfast, a variety of sandwiches, flatbread pizzas, and entrées for lunch, and a killer coconut cream pie. Pat herself can sometimes be found bussing tables. There's also a cafeteria-style restaurant.

Kitchen Kettle Village is home base to **AAA Buggy Rides** (717/989-2829, www.aaabuggy rides.com, 9 A.M.–6 P.M. Mon.–Sat. weather permitting), which offers a 55-minute excursion ($16, children 3–12 $8) that goes through a covered bridge as well as a 35-minute trip ($12, children $6). Reservations aren't required. The village also features pony rides, a petting zoo, and a playground. Want to stick around after it closes to the public? **The Inn at Kitchen Kettle Village** ($89–199) offers a variety of lodging options, including standard rooms in small cottages with yards and porches and suites that sleep up to six. Rates include breakfast at the Kling House every day except Sunday. Book well in advance if you're coming for the **Rhubarb Festival** (third weekend in May), the **Berry Jam Festival** (third weekend in June), or another of the village's annual events.

Landis Valley Museum

Born two years apart in the 1860s, brothers Henry and George Landis had a lot in common. Both became engineers. Neither married. They were the kind of people who never threw anything away—the kind who collected things other people regarded as valueless. By 1925 the brothers had amassed so many objects

reflective of Pennsylvania German rural life that they opened a small museum on their homestead a few miles north of downtown Lancaster, charging visitors 25 cents apiece. They died a year apart in the 1950s, but the museum (2451 Kissel Hill Rd., Lancaster, 717/569-0401, www.landisvalleymuseum.org, 9 A.M.–5 P.M. Mon.–Sat., noon–5 P.M. Sun., admission $12, seniors $10, children 3–11 $8) lives on. Owned by the state since 1953, it has grown into an assemblage of 30-plus historic and recreated buildings housing a collection of more than 100,000 farm, trade, and household artifacts. While some historic buildings are original to the site, including the Landis brothers' 1870s house, many were relocated here over the years. They include a blacksmith shop, a circa 1800 log building that houses exhibits on early printing and leatherworking, and a late 1800s schoolhouse complete with authentic furnishings. Rather than a time capsule of a particular era, Landis Valley is a repository for all things illustrative of PA Dutch village and farm life from the mid-1700s to mid-1900s. Costumed interpreters are often on

© ANNA DUBROVSKY

the Landis Valley Museum

hand to demonstrate skills such as open-hearth cooking, horse-drawn plowing, tinsmithing, woodcarving, and weaving. Heirloom gardens and heritage breed farm animals help bring the past to life. Be sure to stop by the museum store, which features traditional handicrafts.

Landis Valley Museum shares a parking lot with **Hands-on House** (721 Landis Valley Rd., Lancaster, 717/569-5437, www.handsonhouse.org, 10 A.M.–5 P.M. Mon.–Thurs. and Sat., 10 A.M.–8 P.M. Fri., noon–5 P.M. Sun. Memorial Day–Labor Day, 11 A.M.–4 P.M. Tues.–Thurs., 11 A.M.–8 P.M. Fri., 10 A.M.–5 P.M. Sat., noon–5 P.M. Sun. Labor Day–Memorial Day, admission $7), a museum designed for children 2–10.

Hans Herr House

Built in 1719, the Hans Herr House (1849 Hans Herr Dr., Willow St., 717/464-4438, www.hansherr.org, 9 A.M.–4 P.M. Mon.–Sat. Apr.–Nov., tour $5, children 7–12 $2) is the oldest structure in Lancaster County and the oldest Mennonite meetinghouse in the western hemisphere. Though named for the Mennonite bishop whose flock established the first permanent European settlement in present-day Lancaster County, the stone house was actually built by his son Christian. The younger Herr was also a bishop, and worship services were held in his Germanic abode. It was home to several generations of the family until the 1860s, after which it was used as a barn and storage shed. Today it's the centerpiece of a museum complex that also includes two 19th-century Pennsylvania German farmhouses, several barns and other outbuildings, and a collection of farm equipment spanning three centuries. You can explore the grounds at your own pace—for free—but must be accompanied by a guide inside the Hans Herr House, restored and furnished to reflect the period 1719–1750. The last house tour begins at 3:15 P.M. Aficionados of 20th-century American art may recognize its exterior. The great Andrew Wyeth, a descendant of Hans Herr, captured the house on canvas before its restoration.

National Watch & Clock Museum

The largest and most comprehensive horological collection in North America can be found in the river town of Columbia, about 10 miles west of Lancaster. I know what you're thinking: "horo-huh?" Horology is the science of measuring time. Sounds like staid stuff, but a visit to the National Watch & Clock Museum (514 Poplar St., Columbia, 717/684-8261, www.nawcc.org, 10 A.M.–4 P.M. Tues.–Sat. Dec.–Mar., 10 A.M.–5 P.M. Tues.–Sat. and noon–4 P.M. Sun. Apr.–Nov., also open Mondays Memorial Day–Labor Day, admission $8, seniors $7, children 5–16 $4, family $20) will convince you otherwise. Located in the world headquarters of the National Association of Watch and Clock Collectors, the museum traces the history of timekeeping from ancient times to present day. Sundials, it turns out, weren't the only timepieces in the days before mechanical clocks. Learn how bowls of water, candles, oil lamps, and incense were used to measure the passage of time. The museum's tick-tocking treasures include early English tall-case clocks, enchanting German musical clocks, vintage and modern wristwatches, and pocket watches spanning three centuries, including one carried by Caroline Bonaparte, youngest sister of Napoleon I. Its collection, which has grown to more than 12,000 items, is strongest in 19th-century American clocks and watches. The doozy: a so-called monumental clock made in Hazleton, Pennsylvania, by one Stephen Engle. Designed to awe and amuse audiences, monumental clocks had their heyday in the late 19th century, touring the United States and Europe like so many modern rock stars. Engle spent more than 20 years crafting his 11-foot-tall clock, which has 48 moving figurines and can display such information as month, day of the week, and moon phase along with time. Finishing it around 1878, he entrusted it to promoters who touted it as "The Eighth Wonder of the World" as they hauled it around the eastern U.S., charging adults a quarter and children 15 cents to see it. In 1951, after an appearance at the Ohio State Fair, the clock vanished. Members of

© ANNA DUBROVSKY

the National Watch & Clock Museum

the National Association of Watch and Clock Collectors spent years hunting for it, finally discovering it in a barn in 1988. Museum staff animate the clock at the top of each hour. The eclectic cast of characters that emerge from its three towers includes Jesus and Satan, three Marys and the 12 apostles, Revolutionary War soldiers and paragon of bravery Molly Pitcher, and Engle himself.

Lititz

In a county studded with lovely little towns, Lititz is generally regarded as the loveliest one of all. The clip-clop of Amish buggies that contributes so much to the appeal of Bird-in-Hand, Intercourse, Strasburg, and other communities west of Lancaster is rarely heard in Lititz. What draws visitors to the borough nine miles north of downtown Lancaster is a combination of historical ambience, boutique shopping, and a busy calendar of events. It doesn't hurt that the smell of chocolate wafts through the streets.

Most of the shops, galleries, eateries, and landmarks lie along East Main Street (Route 772) or Broad Street (Route 501), which meet in the center of town. Be aware that many are closed on Sundays. The second Friday of the month is a great day to visit because merchants pull out all the stops for **Lovin' Lititz Every 2nd** (717/626-6332, www.lititzpa.com, 5–9 P.M.), featuring free entertainment and free parking throughout town. Lititz is also a great place to be on Independence Day. First held in 1818, the **Fourth of July Celebration** (717/626-8981, www.lititzspringspark.org, admission charged) in Lititz Springs Park is the oldest continuous observance of the national holiday. The daylong festivities conclude with the lighting of 7,000 candles and a fireworks show.

Lititz boasts a unique history. It was founded in 1756 by members of the Moravian Church, an evangelical Protestant denomination that originated in the modern-day Czech Republic. For almost 100 years, only Moravians were permitted to live in the village. A group of strict church elders oversaw all aspects of day-to-day

© ANNA DUBROVSKY

historic Lititz

life, calling the shots in economic as well as religious matters. After opening its doors to outsiders in the 1850s, Lititz became a stop on the Reading and Columbia Railroad and a summer resort area. Lititz Springs Park and the limestone springs that give it its name were the main attraction. A replica of the passenger depot that stood at the entrance to the park from 1884 to 1957 houses the **Lititz Welcome Center** (18 N. Broad St., 717/626-8981, www .lititzspringspark.org, 10 A.M.–4 P.M. Mon.– Sat. and until 8 P.M. on the second Fri. of the month). On the opposite side of the train tracks, which are still used for moving freight, is the **Wilbur Chocolate Company** (48 N. Broad St., 717/626-3249, www.wilburbuds .com, store and museum open 10 A.M.–5 P.M. Mon.–Sat., free admission). Founded in 1884 in Philadelphia, based in Lititz since the 1930s, and owned by agribusiness conglomerate Cargill since 1992, Wilbur manufactures chocolate and other ingredients for the baking, candy, and dairy industries. It's best known to consumers for chocolates that resemble a

flower bud. (Wilbur Buds also bear a striking resemblance to Hershey's Kisses, which at more than 100 years old aren't quite as old as the squatter Buds.) The factory store offers free samples of the signature confection and a wide selection of other goodies, including fudge, marshmallows, almond bark, and peanut butter meltaways made on the spot. The attached Candy Americana Museum showcases antique candy machinery, cocoa tins, chocolate molds and boxes, marble slabs and rolling pins, and more than 150 porcelain chocolate pots from around the world.

As if sweet tooths needed another reason to visit Lititz, a chocolate-centric eatery opened in 2005. **Café Chocolate of Lititz** (40 E. Main St., 717/626-0123, www.chocolatelititz.com, 10 A.M.–5 P.M. Sun.–Thurs., 9 A.M.–9 P.M. Fri.–Sat., $6–10) is all about dark chocolate, eschewing varieties with less than 50 percent cocoa solids. Owner Selina Man also eschews foods with preservatives, buying organic whenever possible. The menu is short but varied, representing several cuisines. That makes choosing a wine or beer to bring to the BYOB a bit tricky: What pairs well with chocolate-drizzled crepes, mulligatawny soup, *and* "chili con chocolate" with smoked turkey or vegan sausage? A chocolate fountain in the front window reminds passersby of the house specialty: a $20 chocolate fondue for two (or even four).

The food lover's tour of Lititz doesn't end there. Just a couple of blocks from Café Chocolate is the **Julius Sturgis Pretzel Bakery** (219 E. Main St., 717/626-4354, www .juliussturgis.com, store 10 A.M.–4 P.M. Mon.–Fri. and 9 A.M.–5 P.M. Sat. Jan.–mid-Mar., 9 A.M.–5 P.M. Mon.–Sat. mid-Mar.–Dec., tour $3, children $2). Established in 1861, it's regarded as America's first pretzel bakery. Tours are offered from a half hour before the bakery store opens to a half hour before it closes and include a hands-on lesson in pretzel twisting. The bakery, with its original brick ovens, doesn't do a whole lot of baking these days. Soft pretzels are made in-house, but the many varieties of hard pretzels available in the store come from Tom Sturgis Pretzels, a Reading-area bakery founded by Julius's grandson.

The sturdy stone house that Julius turned into a pretzel bakery was built in 1784. It's one of more than a dozen 18th-century buildings still in use on East Main Street. Another houses the **Lititz Museum** (145 E. Main St., 717/627-4636, www.lititzhistoricalfounda tion.com, 10 A.M.–4 P.M. Mon.–Sat. Memorial Day–last Sat. in Oct. and Fri.–Sat. Nov.–Sat. before Christmas, free admission), the place to go for a primer on the town's history. The Lititz Historical Foundation, which operates the museum, offers tours of the neighboring **Johannes Mueller House** (admission $5, seniors $4, high school students $3) from Memorial Day through the last Saturday in October. Built in 1792, the stone house remains practically unchanged and is furnished with hundreds of artifacts from the late 1700s and early 1800s. Tours are led by costumed guides and take approximately 45 minutes.

Wolf Sanctuary of Pennsylvania

Despite its official-sounding name, the Wolf Sanctuary (465 Speedwell Forge Rd., Lititz, 717/626-4617, www.wolfsancpa.com) is not a state facility. It's the pet project of one Lancaster County family, the Darlingtons, with a lot of land and a love for the animal portrayed so harshly in fairy tales. The Darlingtons began taking in wolves and wolf hybrids in the 1980s, after the state forbade keeping them as house pets. Today about 40 onetime pets—who can't be released into the wild because they rely on humans for food—roam 20-odd acres of the family's property. Public tours of the fenced refuge are offered Tuesdays, Thursdays, Saturdays, and Sundays. Reservations are required for the weekday tours, which start at 10 A.M. and cost $15 per adult, $14 per senior, and $13 per child 12 and under. You can just show up for weekend tours, offered at 10 A.M. June–September and noon October–May. They're $12 per adult, $11 per seniors, and $10 per child. Once a month, on the Saturday closest to the full moon, the sanctuary is open to the public in the evening. By the Light of the Moon tours (7:30–10 P.M., $20 per person, reservations requested), closed to children under 16, feature a campfire and live acoustical music. Private tours are available by appointment and cost $25 per person. The tours are a bit of a hike, so dress accordingly. It's best to visit during cold weather, which wolves prefer. On hot days Blazer, Frodo, Kojac, and other sanctuary residents are loath to emerge from holes they dig beneath their shelters.

If you're interested in spending hours or even days with the wolves, you're in luck. In 2005 the Darlingtons opened a B&B on their 100-plus acre property, which was the site of an iron forge from the 1760s to 1850s. **Speedwell Forge B&B** (717/626-1760 www .speedwellforge.com, $125–250) offers three guest rooms in what used to be the ironmaster's mansion and two private cottages. Grandest of them all is the Paymaster's Office cottage, so named because it's where forge employees were paid. The honeymoon-worthy retreat boasts a vaulted ceiling, massive brick fireplace, king-sized bed, and in-room whirlpool bath. The former paymaster's window separates the main room from a kitchenette. A less expensive alternative for romantics is the mansion's master bedroom, featuring a canopy bed and claw-foot whirlpool bath for two.

Ephrata Cloister

The town of Ephrata, about 15 miles north of downtown Lancaster, is best known as the onetime home of a religious community whose faithful ate meager rations and slept on wooden benches with blocks of wood for pillows. The Ephrata Cloister (632 W. Main St., Ephrata, 717/733-6600, 9 A.M.–5 P.M. Mon.–Sat., noon–5 P.M. Sun., closed Mon. and Tues. Jan.–Feb., admission $9, seniors $8, children 3–11 $6) was the hub of their community and home to members who chose a celibate life. The buildings where white-robed Brothers and Sisters lived, worked, and prayed in the 1700s are now open to the public.

Their leader, Conrad Beissel, was born in Germany in 1691. As a young man he was drawn to Pietism, a movement by religious purists to reform the state-supported Protestant churches. Banished from his homeland, he immigrated to Pennsylvania like so many German pietists drawn by William Penn's promise of religious freedom. In 1724 he was tapped to lead a newly formed German Baptist Brethren congregation, where his promotion of celibacy and other radical ideas caused a fissure. He left the church and in 1732 settled along the banks of the Cocalico Creek in northern Lancaster County to lead a hermit's life. Hermit-hood was not to be. The charismatic theologian was soon joined by followers, and their settlement became known as Ephrata, a biblical reference. At its zenith in the mid-1800s, the community consisted of about 80 celibate members and 200 "householders" who lived on farms around the Cloister. The community became known for its Germanic calligraphy, publishing center, and original a cappella music. Beissel prescribed a special diet for members of the choir, who sang at an otherworldly high pitch. Today the music composed by Beissel and crew is performed by the Ephrata Cloister Chorus at occasional concerts.

Beissel died in 1768 and was buried in a graveyard on the cloister grounds. His successor wasn't married to the idea of monastic life. After the death of the last celibate member in 1813, householders formed the German Seventh Day Baptist Church. The congregation disbanded in 1934, and several years later the state purchased the Cloister property, now a National Historic Landmark. Some of the original buildings, including a worship hall known as the saal, can only be viewed during guided tours, which are offered daily. You can explore other structures on your own.

ENTERTAINMENT AND EVENTS
Concert Venues

American Music Theatre (2425 Lincoln Highway East, Lancaster, 717/397-7700, www.amtshows.com) has presented concerts by Joe Cocker, Vince Gill, The Beach Boys, The B-52s, Huey Lewis and the News, Melissa Etheridge, Clay Aiken, and a host of other big-name entertainers since opening in 1997. It produces a handful of original shows each year, including a glitzy Christmas revue. The 1,600-seat theater is across U.S. 30 from the Rockvale Outlets.

Performing Arts

Downtown Lancaster is home to one of the oldest theaters in the country. Built in 1852 on the foundation of a pre-Revolutionary prison, the **Fulton Theatre** (12 N. Prince St., Lancaster, 717/397-7425, www.thefulton.org) hosted lectures by Mark Twain and Horace Greeley, performances by Sarah Bernhardt and W. C. Fields, a production of *Ben-Hur* featuring live horses in a spectacular chariot-racing scene (fistfights broke out at the box office when tickets went on sale), and burlesque in its first 100 years. In the 1950s and '60s it served primarily as a movie house. Since then the Fulton has reinvented itself as a producer of professional theater. Productions range from small-cast plays such as *Doubt* to beloved musicals such as *Les Misérables* and *Hello, Dolly!* Each season features a handful

© CICERO DONNELLY

Fulton Theatre in downtown Lancaster

of shows designed for pint-sized theater-goers. The auditorium, which seats about 700, was restored to its original Victorian splendor in 1995. It's one of a dwindling number still using sandbags and hemp ropes to move scenery. A 100-seat studio theater added during the $9.5 million renovation and expansion is used for an annual cabaret series. Named for a Lancaster County native credited with developing the first commercially successful steamboat, the Fulton is the primary venue of the professional **Lancaster Symphony Orchestra** (www .lancastersymphony.org).

Lancaster County has not one but two dinner theaters. In business since 1984, **Rainbow Dinner Theatre** (3065 Lincoln Highway East, Paradise, 800/292-4301, www.rainbow dinnertheatre.com) bills itself as America's only all-comedy dinner theater. It produces four knee-slappers per year, including a Christmas-themed show. The **Dutch Apple Dinner** **Theatre** (510 Centerville Rd., Lancaster, 717/898-1900, www.dutchapple.com) serves up more shows, and its menu includes dramatic fare such as *Rent.* Both offer buffet-style dining. The theaters are set back from the road and easily missed. Rainbow is behind the Best Western Revere Inn & Suites on U.S. 30, about three miles east of the Rockvale Outlets. The Dutch Apple shares a driveway with the Heritage Hotel—Lancaster, just off the Centerville exit of U.S. 30.

Sight & Sound Theatres

With two theaters in Lancaster County and a third in Branson, Missouri, Sight & Sound (800/377-1277, www.sight-sound.com) is the nation's largest Christian theatrical company. Founded in the 1970s by a Lancaster County native, it pulls out all the stops to dramatize biblical stories such as Noah's wet and wild journey, Joseph's journey from slavery to

a scene from *Joseph*, at the Sight & Sound's Millennium Theatre

© SIGHT & SOUND THEATRES

power, and the birth of Jesus. Think elaborate sets and special effects, professional actors and live animals. The Lancaster County theaters are a half mile apart along Route 896, between U.S. 30 and the town of Strasburg. Larger of the two, the **Millennium Theatre** (300 Hartman Bridge Rd., Ronks) is a vision inside and out. The sprawling, pastel-hued palace features three exterior domes (representing the Trinity), a wraparound stage double the size of Radio City Music Hall's, and the largest moving light system on the East Coast. Four-legged cast members amble to their spots—and "dressing rooms"—via specially designed passageways under the theater floor. Behind-the-scenes tours, offered March through October, are nearly as fascinating as the productions. The 643-seat **Living Waters Theatre** (202 Hartman Bridge Rd., Ronks) is Sight & Sound's original home.

Festivals and Events

What started in 1980 as a jousting demo to draw attention to a new winery has grown into one of Pennsylvania Dutch Country's marquee attractions. Jousting is just the tip of the lance at the **Pennsylvania Renaissance Faire** (2775 Lebanon Rd., Manheim, 717/665-7021, www.parenfaire.com, admission charged), which brings some 250,000 people to Mount Hope Estate & Winery over the course of 12 weekends from early August to late October. Transported to Elizabethan England, Fairegoers party like it's 1589 alongside sword swallowers and fire breathers, magicians and musicians, jugglers and jesters. The Ren Faire features more than 70 shows per day, including performances of Shakespeare's plays in a three-story replica of London's Globe Theatre. Human pawns, knights, and bishops battle it out on a 40-foot-by-40-foot chessboard. Merchants in period costumes demonstrate glassblowing, pottery throwing, leather working, bow and arrow making, and more. Even the food vendors wear the clothes and talk the talk of Shakespeare's day as they serve up everything from gelato to giant turkey legs. "Drynke" options include wine, mead, beer, and soft drinks made on-site. Admission is $29.95 for adults, $9.95 for children 5–11. Buy tickets online for savings of $5 per adult ticket. Though best known for the Ren Faire, Mount Hope Estate hosts a variety of entertainment throughout the year, including improv comedy, murder mystery dinners, and a Celtic festival. Located 15 miles north of Lancaster, the National Register–listed property was home to a prominent iron-making family in the 19th century.

Lancaster's Long's Park (1441 Harrisburg Pike, Lancaster, 717/735-8883, www.longs park.org) is another site of much merrymaking. The city park just off U.S. 30 is a poultry-lover's paradise on the third Saturday of May, when the Sertoma Club of Lancaster holds its annual fund-raiser for the park. Members of the civic organization serve more than 30,000 chicken dinners over the course of eight hours. The **Sertoma Chicken BBQ** (717/354-7259, www.lancastersertomabbq.com, tickets $8 in advance, $9 at the park), a tradition since 1953, held the Guinness World Record for most meat consumed at an outdoor event for more than a decade, losing it to a Paraguayan shindig in 2008. June marks the start of the **Long's Park Summer Music Series** (7:30 P.M. Sun. June–Aug.), another decades-old tradition. Bring blankets, lawn chairs, and nibbles for the free concerts. Alcohol isn't permitted in the 80-acre park. The music series is funded in part by proceeds from the **Long's Park Art & Craft Festival** (one-day tickets $8 in advance, $10 at the park), held over Labor Day weekend. The four-day festival showcases the work of 200 artists and craftspeople from across the country.

SHOPPING
Outlet Malls

Lancaster County's two outlet malls are just a couple of minutes apart on U.S. 30. **Rockvale Outlets** (35 S. Willowdale Dr., Lancaster, 717/293-9595, www.rockvalesquare outlets.com, 9:30 A.M.–9 P.M. Mon.–Sat., 11 A.M.–5 P.M. Sun.) features about 100 stores, including Lane Bryant, Jones New York,

Pendleton, Casual Male XL, Izod, Gymboree, and Disney Store. It's a great place to shop for the home, counting Pottery Barn, Restoration Hardware, Lenox, and Corningware Corelle Revere among its tenants.

Tanger Outlet Center (311 Stanley K. Tanger Blvd., Lancaster, 717/392-7260, www .tangeroutlet.com, 9 A.M.–9 P.M. Mon.–Sat., 10 A.M.–6 P.M. Sun.), located across U.S. 30 from Dutch Wonderland amusement park, is smaller but chicer, offering designer brands such as Polo Ralph Lauren, Kenneth Cole, Calvin Klein, Brooks Brothers, Coach, and Movado.

"Antiques Capital USA"

Located just off exit 286 of the Pennsylvania Turnpike, the little burg of Adamstown has made a big name for itself in antiquing circles. The self-proclaimed antiques capital of the United States is crowded with antiques shops, malls, and markets, most of which can be found along North Reading Road (Route 272). Sundays are a big day in "Antiques Capital USA" (www.antiquescapital.com). That's when **Renninger's Antiques Market** and the **Black Angus Antiques Mall** are open. The former (2500 N. Reading Rd., 717/336-2177, www.renningers.com, indoor market 7:30 A.M.–4 P.M. Sun., outdoor market opens at 5 A.M.) features upwards of 300 booths indoors and, weather permitting, hundreds more outdoors. Bring a flashlight to get in on the early morning action. The 70,000-square-foot Black Angus Antiques Mall (2800 N. Reading Rd., 717/484-4386, www.stoudts.com, mall 7:30 A.M.–4 P.M. Sun., outdoor pavilions 5 A.M.–noon) is part of a sprawling complex of businesses operated by husband and wife Ed and Carol Stoudt. More than 300 dealers set up shop in the mall, selling everything from fine art and early American furniture to tools and small collectibles. Outdoor pavilions accommodate about 100 more.

At 1 P.M., take a break from shopping for a free tour of **Stoudt's Brewing Company.** Frequent visitors to Europe, the Stoudts established the microbrewery in 1987 with the goal of making an authentic German-style beer. And they succeeded: Gold Lager and Pils, the brewery's German-style flagship beers, have racked up awards and accolades. Its top seller, however, is an American pale ale sold in bottles emblazoned with the stars and stripes. Brewery tours, also offered at 3 P.M. Saturdays, meet in the lobby of the adjacent **Black Angus Restaurant & Pub** (4:30–10 P.M. Mon.–Thurs., noon–10 P.M. Fri.–Sat., 11:30 A.M.–8 P.M. Sun., dining room menu $18–39, pub menu $9–19), a.k.a. "the house that beef built." The antiques-filled eatery has specialized in steaks since Ed Stoudt opened it in 1962. All dinners are served with bread made in the **Wonderful Good Market** (9 A.M.–5 P.M. Fri.–Sat., 7:30 A.M.–3 P.M. Sun.), the Stoudts' bakery, creamery, and specialty foods store.

Adamstown offers plenty of antiquing on days other than Sunday. **Heritage Antique Center** (2750 N. Reading Rd., 717/484-4646, www.heritageantiquecenter.com), one of the area's oldest antiques stores, and the **Antiques Showcase & German Trading Post** (2152 N.

Reading Rd., 717/336-8847, www.blackhorse lodge.com), with nearly 300 showcases full of fine antiques and investment-grade collectibles, are open 10 A.M.–5 P.M. seven days a week. Not to be missed if you visit on a weekend: **The Country French Collection** (2887 N. Reading Rd., 717/484-0200, www.countryfrench antiques.com, noon–4 P.M. Fri.–Sun. and by appointment), which imports 18th- and 19th-century antiques from France and England and restores them to pristine condition.

For several days every April, June, and September, Adamstown's antiquing scene goes into overdrive. Outside markets mushroom and inside markets keep longer hours during the **Antiques Extravaganzas,** which attract dealers from across the country.

Mud Sales

Held at fire companies throughout Lancaster County, "mud sales" are a chance to get dirt-cheap prices on everything from antiques to aluminum siding, lawn equipment to livestock, homemade food to horse carriages. Teeming as they are with Amish and Mennonite buyers

Mud sales, named for the condition of the thawing spring ground, are held annually throughout Lancaster County to benefit local fire companies.

and sellers, these fund-raising sales/auctions are also a cultural immersion experience. Why are they called mud sales? Because most take place between mid-February and mid-April, when the ground is thawing—though it's not unheard of for fire companies to hold mud sales in the middle of summer. Visit www.padutch country.com or call 717/299-8901 for a schedule of sales, which begin bright and early.

Quilts and Fabrics

Mud sales are great places to buy locally crafted quilts, but if your visit to Lancaster County doesn't coincide with one, you're not out of luck. Quilt shops are more common than stoplights in the Amish countryside. Most sell a variety of handicrafts. (This author's fave: the ingenious pillow-blanket hybrid known as the "quillow.") Many are home-based businesses, allowing shoppers a glimpse into the everyday lives of locals. Just about all quilt shops are closed on Sundays. The **Quilt Shop at Miller's** (2811 Lincoln Highway East, Ronks, 717/687-8439, www.quiltshopatmillers.com, 10 A.M.–8 P.M. daily June–Aug., 10 A.M.–7 P.M. Mon.–Sat. and 10 A.M.–6 P.M. Sun. Sept.–Dec. and Apr.–May, 10 A.M.–5 P.M. Wed.–Sun. Jan.–Feb.) is an exception. It's right next to the popular Miller's Smorgasbord on U.S. 30, about a mile and a half east of Route 896.

Intercourse is a good place to start a quilt-shopping spree. The village along Route 340 (Old Philadelphia Pike) is home to **The People's Place Quilt Museum** (3510 Old Philadelphia Pike, Intercourse, 800/828-8218, www.ppquiltmuseum.com, 9 A.M.–5 P.M. Mon.–Sat., free admission), which is best known for showcasing antique Amish and Mennonite quilts but has also mounted exhibitions of contemporary quilts, African American quilts, and antebellum album quilts since its 1988 opening. The museum store is a trove of folk art from around the country. You'll find miniature quilts created with antique fabrics, loom-woven wool table runners, dolls with patchwork skirts and tiny accessories, Shaker boxes, wire-wrap jewelry, and more. The museum occupies the second floor of **The Old**

Country Store (800/828-8218, www.theold countrystore.com, 9 A.M.–6:30 P.M. Mon.–Sat. June–Aug., 9 A.M.–5 P.M. Mon.–Sat. Sept.–May), stocked with thousands of items made by local craftspeople, most of them Amish or Mennonite. In addition to hundreds of quilts, it carries potholders and pottery, Christmas ornaments and cornhusk bunnies, faceless Amish dolls and darling stuffed bears, pillows of various sizes and paper cuttings known as *scherenschnitte*. With its selection of more than 6,000 bolts of fabric, the store is as much a starting point for needlecraft projects as a showplace for finished products. Quilt books, color-coordinated fabric packs, and pattern kits are also on offer.

In the complex of shops known as Kitchen Kettle Village is the airy **Village Quilts** (3529 Old Philadelphia Pike, Intercourse, 717/768-2787, www.kitchenkettle.com/quilts, 9 A.M.–5 P.M. Mon.–Sat.), which commissions works from a select group of home quilters. Each masterpiece is signed and dated and comes with a certificate for insurance purposes. The shop offers one-on-one quilting instruction ($80 for 90 minutes) by appointment. It can also arrange for a professional quilter to hop in your car and accompany you to other area shops. Call at least two weeks in advance to book a **Quilt Shop Hop** (10 A.M. Mon.–Fri., $150 for 2 people, $25 per additional person), which includes a stop for lunch.

A few minutes east of Intercourse along Route 340 is **Esh's Handmade Quilts** (3829 Old Philadelphia Pike, Gordonville, 717/768-8435, 9 A.M.–6 P.M. Mon.–Sat.), a small shop on a family dairy farm. And a few minutes west of Intercourse is **The Quilt & Fabric Shack** (3137 Old Philadelphia Pike, Bird-In-Hand, 717/768-0338, www.thequiltandfabricshack .com, 9 A.M.–5 P.M. Mon.–Sat.), boasting a large selection of quilts made by local Amish and Mennonites and four rooms of all-cotton fabrics. Its bargain room features some 700 bolts priced at $3 per yard. Just northwest of Intercourse along Route 772, **Family Farm Quilts** (3511 W. Newport Rd., 717/768-8375, www.familyfarmquilts.com, 9 A.M.–5 P.M.

Mon.–Sat.) counts more than 200 local women among its quilt suppliers. Its selection of handicrafts includes purses made of antique quilts, placemats, chair pads, children's toys, and baskets.

Witmer Quilt Shop (1070-76 W. Main St., New Holland, 717/656-9526, 8 A.M.–8 P.M. Mon. and Fri., 8 A.M.–6 P.M. Tues.–Thurs. and Sat.), located five miles north of Intercourse along Route 23, is remarkable for its selection of lovingly restored antique quilts. Emma Witmer's shop/home is also stocked with more than 100 new quilts, many in patterns she herself designed. Give her a few months and she'll give you a custom quilt. Drive less than half a mile west on Route 23 and turn right onto North Groffdale Road to reach the Amish dairy farm that's home to **Smuckers Quilts** (117 N. Groffdale Rd., New Holland, 717/656-8730, 8 A.M.–8 P.M. Mon.–Sat.), specializing in traditional patterns. A left onto South Groffdale will bring you to the Amish poultry farm that's home to **Country Lane Quilts** (221 S. Groffdale Rd., Leola, 717/656-8476, 8:30 A.M.–5 P.M. Mon.–Sat.). If you continue past Groffdale, make a left at Hess Road and a right at East Eby Road, you'll arrive at yet another Amish dairy farm with a handicrafts biz: **Riehl's Quilts and Crafts** (247 E. Eby Rd., Leola, 800/957-7105, www.riehlsamishquilts.com, 8 A.M.–5 P.M. Mon.–Sat.).

As you make your way between the shops, each carrying quilts by dozens if not hundreds of local women, keep your eyes peeled for handmade "quilts sold here" signs inviting you to pull into a drive and knock on the door.

Susquehanna Glass Factory Outlet and Tour

Founded in 1910, Susquehanna Glass (731 Ave. H, Columbia, 717/684-2155, www.susquehannaglass.com, store open 9 A.M.–5 P.M. Tues.–Sat., tours 10:30 A.M. and 1 P.M. Tues. and Thurs., reservations required) counts retailers Williams-Sonoma, Restoration Hardware, and David's Bridal among its customers. The glass decorator best known for personalized products offers everything from storage jars to lead crystal bowls at its factory store, located half a mile from the National Watch & Clock Museum in the Susquehanna River town of Columbia. Tours of the factory, where glass is still cut by hand, are offered year-round except when temps creep into the 90s. The tours are free and last 30–45 minutes.

SPORTS AND RECREATION
Spectator Sports

Professional baseball returned to Lancaster in 2005, 44 years after the Lancaster Red Roses folded. Named the **Lancaster Barnstormers** (Clipper Magazine Stadium, 650 N. Prince St., Lancaster, 717/509-3633, www.lancasterbarnstormers.com) by popular vote, the team swept its way to an Atlantic League championship in only its second season. Nearby York was added to the league the following year, and the two cities rekindled their historical "War of the Roses" rivalry. (Back when Lancaster had the Red Roses, York had the White Roses. York's modern-day club is called the Revolution.) Their mayors agreed that the loser of the season-long war would plant a rose garden at the victor's stadium. Clipper Magazine Stadium, built for the Barnstormers, is the first ballpark to boast a bumper boat pond.

Monster truck showdowns, demolition derbies, and other high-octane spectacles bring families to **Buck Motorsports Park** (900 Lancaster Pike, Quarryville, 800/344-7855, www.buckmotorsports.com) on Saturday evenings from May to early October. "The Buck" is 10 miles south of Lancaster on Route 272.

ACCOMMODATIONS

Lancaster County has lodging options aplenty. Its hotels and motels run the gamut from major brands such as Holiday Inn, Comfort Inn, and Travelodge to unique independents such as the **Red Caboose** (312 Paradise Ln., Ronks, 717/687-5000, www.redcaboosemotel.com, $69–159), a motel made of restored railroad cars, and the 97-room **Fulton Steamboat Inn** (Routes 30 and 896, Lancaster, 717/299-9999, www.fultonsteamboatinn.com, $80–180), built to resemble a steamboat and named

© ANNA DUBROVSKY

Sleep in a restored railroad car at the Red Caboose.

for a Lancaster County native who pioneered steam-powered shipping. Travelers who prefer bed-and-breakfasts can take their pick of more than 150. Indeed, Lancaster County has more B&Bs than any place on the Eastern Seaboard except Cape Cod. They're a diverse bunch: Bed down in an 18th-century stone house, an elegant Victorian manse, or on a working farm. If you travel with young children, you probably eschew B&Bs, but a farm stay is a different animal (hardy har har). It's lodging, education, and entertainment rolled into one—assuming your kids find gathering eggs and bottle-feeding calves entertaining. A list of Lancaster County farms that offer overnight accommodations is available at www.afarmstay.com.

The **Pennsylvania Dutch Convention & Visitors Bureau** (717/299-8901, www.padutchcountry.com) is a great source of information about lodging options. Its website allows for searches by price range and lodging type. The **Mennonite Information Center** (2209 Millstream Rd., Lancaster, 717/299-0954, www.mennoniteinfoctr.com),

best known for its personal tours of the Amish countryside, maintains a list of Mennonite-owned guesthouses, available at the center and on its website.

Under $100

Families can spend the night at **Old Mill Stream Campground** (2249 Lincoln Hwy. E., Lancaster, 717/299-2314, www.oldmillstreamcampground.com, $33–43) for a fraction of what it costs to spend the day at the adjacent Dutch Wonderland amusement park. The 15-acre campground, which Hershey Entertainment & Resorts purchased along with Dutch Wonderland in 2001, has more than 160 tent and RV sites open year-round. Amenities include a 24-hour game room, a country store, laundry rooms, and free wireless Internet access.

The **Carriage House Motor Inn** (144 E. Main St., Strasburg, 717/687-7651, www.amishcountryinns.com/motor, $59–109) is a good non-camping option in this price range. Walking distance from the Railroad Museum of

Pennsylvania and the Strasburg Rail Road, it's ideal for rail fans. Dogs are welcome, provided they don't weigh in at more than 75 pounds. Rooms have cable TV and refrigerators, and rates include a continental breakfast. For about the same price, you can spend the night at nearby **Rayba Acres Farm** (183 Black Horse Rd., Paradise, 717/687-6729, www.raybaacres .com, $83–90) or **Neffdale Farm** (604 Strasburg Rd., Paradise, 717/687-7837, www.neffdalefarm .com, $80), both Mennonite-owned.

$100-150

Located just off U.S. 30 west of Lancaster city, the **Heritage Hotel–Lancaster** (500 Centerville Rd., Lancaster, 800/223-8963, www.heritagelancaster.com, $94–124) is a great choice for nightlife-loving travelers. Its restaurant and bar, **Loxley's** (6:30 A.M.–midnight Sun.–Thurs., 6:30 A.M.–2 A.M. Fri.–Sat., breakfast $3–10, lunch and dinner $9–29) attracts locals and hotel guests alike. Named for Robin of Loxley, the archer and outlaw better known as Robin Hood, it boasts a two-level deck that looks like a giant tree house. In keeping with the legend that inspired it, Loxley's donates 5 percent of food purchases to the needy. The hotel has 166 standard-looking guest rooms, a business center, a fitness room, and an outdoor pool. The Dutch Apple Dinner Theatre is right next door.

Sleep under handmade quilts and awake to the clip-clop of Amish buggies at **The Inn at Kitchen Kettle Village** (3529 Old Philadelphia Pike, Intercourse, 717/768-8261, www.kitchenkettle.com, $89–199). Scattered throughout the uber-quaint village, accommodations range from standard rooms in small cottages with yards and porches to suites that sleep up to six. Breakfast at the on-site Kling House Restaurant is free to inn guests Monday–Saturday.

The Strasburg area, known for its train-related attractions, is also heavily trafficked by Amish buggies. Located in the very center of town, the **Strasburg Village Inn** (1 W. Main St., Strasburg, 717/687-0900, www.strasburg .com, mid-June–Oct. $119–149, Nov.–Mar.

$79–99, Apr.–mid-June $99–119) has 10 classically appointed guest rooms and suites with private baths. The circa 1788 house is outfitted with wireless Internet and flat-screen TVs. Also built in the 1780s, the nearby **Limestone Inn B&B** (33 E. Main St., Strasburg, 717/687-8392, www.thelimestoneinn.com, $99–139) has six guest rooms and traces of a previous life: Wood moldings and doors on the third floor, where ceilings are too low for guests taller than 6 feet, bear the initials of boys who boarded there in the mid-1800s while studying at the then-famous Strasburg Academy. (Ceilings in the spacious second floor rooms are plenty high for everyone.) Innkeepers Richard and Denise Waller also own The Iron Horse Inn, an excellent restaurant down the street, so you can safely count on a superb breakfast.

Breakfast at ◖ **Verdant View Farm B&B** (429 Strasburg Rd., Paradise, 717/687-7353, www.verdantview.com, $71–114), one mile east of Strasburg on Route 741, begins with a joining of hands and a rendition of the Johnny Appleseed song (*Oh, the Lord's been good to me . . .*). It's not unusual for two, three, or even four generations of the Ranck family,

Verdant View Farm owner Don Ranck introduces the guests of his B&B to a baby goat.

© ANNA DUBROVSKY

General Sutter Inn

© ANNA DUBROVSKY

which has operated the 118-acre dairy and crop farm for almost a century, to join guests around the table, set with pitchers of raw milk, platters of farm-fresh meat, eggs, and potatoes, and homemade pies. Breakfast isn't the first thing on the menu at Verdant View. Guests can begin the day with a farm tour, complete with opportunities to milk a cow, frolic with kittens, and feed calves, goats, bunnies, and other animals. Overslept? Don't despair. The tour is offered throughout the day, as are tractor-pulled wagon rides and "farmer's apprentice" programs in topics as diverse as making cheese and artificially inseminating cows. (Breakfast and farm experiences aren't offered on Sundays, when the Rancks attend their Mennonite church.) The nine guest rooms, spread between an 1896 farmhouse and the "little white house" down the lane, are nothing fancy. But what it lacks in frills the B&B more than makes up for in hospitality.

The charming town of Lititz has several recommendable accommodations in this price range. Chief among them is the **General Sutter Inn** (14 E. Main St., Lititz, 717/626-2115, www.generalsutterinn.com, $70–189),

offering 16 antique-filled guest rooms and suites. More than 200 years old, the inn took its present name in the 1930s to honor John Augustus Sutter, who established a settlement in California in the 1840s, saw it overrun by gold-seekers, and lived his final years in Lititz. No two rooms are the same, but all feature pillow-top mattresses, down comforters, flat-panel TVs, and wireless Internet. Guests enjoy a complimentary continental breakfast Monday–Friday and $5 off a full breakfast Saturday–Sunday. The **Alden House Bed & Breakfast** (62 E. Main St., Lititz, 717/627-3363, www.aldenhouse.com, $99–149), with seven guest rooms and suites, is another fine choice in the center of town. Breakfast is a multi-course affair.

Over $150

Visitors to downtown Lancaster may find it hard to believe that the **Lancaster Marriott at Penn Square** (25 S. Queen St., Lancaster, 717/239-1600, www.lancastermarriott.com, $139–289) and adjoining Lancaster County Convention Center opened in 2009. The 299-room hotel smack dab in the center of town

Lancaster Marriott at Penn Square

looks mighty historical. That's because developers incorporated the Beaux Arts facade of a shuttered century-old department store into its design. A contemporary aesthetic takes over in the soaring lobby and spacious rooms. The hotel boasts an indoor pool and serenity-peddling spa (717/207-4076, www .mandarinrosespa.com, 10 A.M.–6 P.M. Mon.–Sat.). The on-site **Penn Square Grille and Rendezvous Lounge** (717/207-4033, www .pennsquaregrille.com, breakfast 6:30–11 A.M. Mon.–Fri. and 7–11 A.M. Sat.–Sun., lunch 11 A.M.–2 P.M. daily, dinner 5–10 P.M. Sun.–Thurs. and 5–11 P.M. Fri.–Sat., lounge open 11 A.M.–1 A.M. daily, lunch $9–15, dinner $18–36, lounge menu $8–34) offer contemporary American cuisine and 30 wines by the glass. Central Market, the Fulton Theatre, the Demuth Museum, and other downtown attractions are just a hop, skip, and a jump away. On the downside: Hotel parking is $14 per day ($24 if you go the valet route), and surfing the Web will set you back $12.95 daily.

With its brick walls and wood beams, locally crafted furnishings and flat-screen TVs, art gallery and organic restaurant, the **(Lancaster Arts Hotel** (300 Harrisburg Ave., 717/299-3000, www.lancasterartshotel.com, rooms $149–219, suites $269–359) is the city's hippest lodging property by a mile. "Hip" implies new, but the building itself dates to the late 1800s. Built as a tobacco warehouse, it found a new life as a boutique hotel in 2006. Original works by area artists adorn each of 63 guest rooms and suites, some of which boast in-room whirlpools. Amenities include 24-hour business and fitness centers, bicycle rentals, free parking, and free shuttle service within a five-mile radius of the hotel. Internet access and a continental breakfast are also on the house. **John J. Jeffries** (717/431-3307, www.johnjjeffries .com, restaurant 5:30–10 P.M. Mon.–Sat. and 5:30–9 P.M. Sun., bar 4 P.M.–midnight Mon.–Sat. and 4–11 P.M. Sun., $11–29), the on-site restaurant and lounge, bills itself as the leading consumer of local organic meats and vegetables in central PA. Happy hour is 4–6 P.M. daily.

Located midway between the villages of Intercourse and Bird-in-Hand on Route 340, **(AmishView Inn & Suites** (3125 Old Philadelphia Pike, Bird-in-Hand, 866/735-1600, www.amishviewinn.com, room $114–214, suite $174–424) is right in the heart of Amish country. Rooms on the backside of the hotel boast farmland views, and the sight of Amish children heading to school or a farmer working his fields with horse-drawn equipment isn't unusual. That's not the only thing it has going for it. AmishView has an indoor pool and whirlpool, fitness and arcade rooms open 24/7, and a guest laundry. Its 50 guest rooms and suites feature kitchenettes, mahogany furniture, 27-inch TVs with cable channels, CD and DVD players, and free high-speed Internet access. Suites have fireplaces and/ or whirlpools. A complimentary country breakfast complete with made-to-order omelets and waffles is served every morning. Plain & Fancy Farm Restaurant, one of the region's most popular PA Dutch eateries, is just outside the doors. **The Inn & Spa at Intercourse Village** (3542 Old Philadelphia Pike, Intercourse, 717/768-2626, www.amishcountryinns.com/inn,

© ANNA DUBROVSKY

$159–399), with nine guest rooms and suites, is another upscale option in Amish country. Made for romance, its three "grand suites" feature gas fireplaces, Jacuzzi tubs for two, king-sized beds, and all-cotton bathrobes. Request the Summer House Suite if you're keen on a heart-shaped tub. A five-course breakfast is served by candlelight. Open to the public, the spa (717/768-0555, 9 A.M.–4 P.M. Mon.–Tues., Thurs., and Sat., 9 A.M.–8 P.M. Wed. and Fri.) offers massages, manicures, and other services in a French country setting.

FOOD

Leave your diet at the Lancaster County line. Visiting this corner of the globe without indulging in a Pennsylvania Dutch–style meal is like visiting Disney World and not riding the rides. The cuisine is anything but light, and unless you seek out a restaurant with an à la carte menu (wussy), you're looking at an all-you-can-eat experience. Approach it with the abandon you bring to Thanksgiving dinner. If you're not stuffed to the gills when you leave, you're sort of missing the point. This is the food of hardworking farm families. This is no time to turn down seconds.

It would be unwise to fill up on PA Dutch foods meal after meal, not only because of the effect on your waistline but because Lancaster County has some excellent non-Deutsch eateries. You can find everything from California-style burritos to authentic Cajun cuisine within its borders. The city of Lancaster has experienced a restaurant renaissance over the past decade, and the 2009 completion of a convention center in the heart of downtown augured well for the dining scene.

Pennsylvania Dutch Fare

If you're new to PA Dutch cuisine, you should know a few things. Around here, **chicken pot pie** isn't a pie at all. It's a stew with square-cut egg noodles. A **whoopie pie** isn't a pie either. Think of it as a dessert burger: creamy icing pressed between two bun-shaped cakes. Chocolate cake with white icing is most common, but you'll also encounter variations such

as pumpkin cake with cream cheese icing. The annual **Whoopie Pie Festival** (Hershey Farm Restaurant & Inn, Rte. 896, Strasburg, 717/687-8635, www.whoopiepiefestival.com, third Sat. in Sept., free) features more than 100 varieties. Pennsylvania Dutch Country's most iconic dessert, the **shoofly pie,** is, in fact, a pie with a crumb crust. But it's nothing like the fruit or cream pies served at diners throughout the country. Packed with molasses and brown sugar, the joltingly sweet treat comes in "wet bottom" and "dry bottom" varieties. A wet-bottomed shoofly pie is more gooey and molasses-y than its dry-bottomed cousin. Other regional specialties include egg noodles with browned butter, **chow-chow** (a pickled vegetable relish), **scrapple** (a breakfast food made with pork scraps), and **schnitz un knepp** (a dish consisting of dried apples, dumplings, and ham).

Lancaster County's most popular PA Dutch restaurants generally fall into one of two categories: smorgasbord and family-style. With seating for 1,200 and a seemingly endless array of dishes, **◖ Shady Maple Smorgasbord** (129 Toddy Dr., East Earl, 717/354-8222, www.shady-maple.com/smorgasbord, breakfast 5–10 A.M. Mon.–Sat., lunch 10:45 A.M.–3:15 P.M. Mon.–Fri., dinner 4–8 P.M. Mon.–Fri. and 10:45 A.M.–8 P.M. Sat.) is the behemoth of the bunch. Don't be surprised to find a waiting line. On Saturday evenings it can take upwards of an hour to get seated. You really need to see this place to appreciate its enormity. Along with Pennsylvania Dutch specialties, lunch and dinner buffets feature everything from pizzas to fajitas to cheesesteaks. Save room for 30-odd dessert options. Lunch costs about $12 and dinner $16–22, depending on the day's specials. Seniors enjoy a 10 percent discount, and children 4–10 eat for half price. (Anyone who has recently undergone a gastric bypass operation also gets a discount.) Shady Maple's breakfast buffet ($9–11 per adult) gets high marks from scrapple fans. A breakfast menu ($3–6) is available on weekdays.

Bird-in-Hand Family Restaurant & Smorgasbord (2760 Old Philadelphia Pike, Bird-in-Hand, 717/768-1550, www.bird-in-hand.com, 6 A.M.–8 P.M. Mon.–Sat., breakfast buffet $9, lunch buffet $10–14, dinner buffet $15–17, age-based pricing for children 4–12) offers both menu and smorgasbord dining for breakfast, lunch, and dinner. Its kids' buffet is designed to look like Noah's Ark, complete with stuffed animals peering through the portholes.

Hershey Farm Restaurant (240 Hartman Bridge Rd., Ronks, 717/687-8635, www .hersheyfarm.com, 8 A.M.–8 P.M. Mon.–Fri. and 7 A.M.–8 P.M. Sat.–Sun., closed Sunday evenings and Mondays Nov.–Apr.) also offers a choice of menu or smorgasbord dining. The on-site bakery is famous for its whoopie pies (Hershey Farm hosts the Whoopie Pie Festival) and triple-layer chocolate cake. A chocolate dipping fountain graces the dessert bar on evenings and weekends. **Miller's Smorgasbord** (2811 Lincoln Hwy. East, Ronks, 717/687-6621, www.millerssmorgasbord.com, breakfast from 7:30 A.M. and lunch/dinner from 11:30 A.M. daily Mar.–Dec., call for Jan.–Feb. hours) is unique in that it accepts reservations and serves alcohol. At $7.95, its weekday breakfast buffet is a steal.

◀ Plain & Fancy Farm Restaurant (3121 Old Philadelphia Pike, Bird-in-Hand, 717/768-4400, www.plainandfancyfarm.com, lunch/dinner from 11:30 A.M. daily Mar.–Dec., closed Jan.–Feb.) is Lancaster County's oldest and arguably best destination for family-style dining. Most family-style restaurants in Pennsylvania Dutch Country follow a similar recipe: Guests are seated—often at tables with other parties—and brought platters of food, which are replenished until everyone is sated. Plain & Fancy's "Amish farm feast" ($19 per person, children 4–12 $10) features made-from-scratch fried chicken, baked sausage, chicken pot pie with homemade noodles, real mashed potatoes, and more. The restaurant, which opened in 1959, also offers an à la carte menu (from $8). Its signature dessert, sour cream apple crumb pie, is out of this world. Though it seats 700, you'd be wise to make a reservation.

Good 'N Plenty Restaurant (150 E. Brook Rd., Smoketown, 717/394-7111, www.goodn plenty.com, 11:30 A.M.–8 P.M. Mon.–Sat.) can accommodate more than 600 guests. Choose from a family-style meal ($20 per person,

Good 'N Plenty Restaurant is a great place to have a family-style meal.

children 4–12 $10) at a communal table or a "harvest platter" ($11 per person, children 4–12 $7) with a meat dish, two sides, and dessert, served at a private table. Just south of Bird-in-Hand on Route 896, Good 'N Plenty boasts an on-site bakery and a large gift shop.

Stoltzfus Farm Restaurant (3716 East Newport Rd., Gordonville, 717/768-8156, www.stoltzfusfarmrestaurant.com, 11:30 A.M.–8 P.M. Mon.–Sat. Apr.–Oct. and Fri.–Sat. in Nov., closed Dec.–Mar.), one block east of Intercourse on Route 772, offers family-style dining in a more intimate setting. Amos Stoltzfus and his wife, Mary, began serving meals in their farmhouse in 1968. Their children took over in 1989 and continue to run the show today. The family-style menu ($17 per person, children 4–12 $8) includes sausage made in the on-site butcher shop and homemade ham loaf. An à la carte menu ($5–9) is available 11:30 A.M.–3 P.M.

Lancaster

With close to a dozen cuisines represented under one roof, **Central Market** (23 N. Market St., 717/735-6890, www.centralmarketlancaster.com, 6 A.M.–4 P.M. Tues. and Fri., 6 A.M.–2 P.M. Sat.) is one of downtown Lancaster's most popular lunch spots. You'll find vendors selling everything from made-to-order salads to homemade rice pudding. Ethnic options include Narai Exotic Thai Cuisine (get there early for the hot-selling fresh spring rolls), Señorita Burrita with its own-made salsas and vegetarian chili, and Saife's Middle Eastern Food. The downsides: Central Market is open just three days a week, and seating is limited. Fortunately, some market vendors have other locations. The original **Señorita Burrita** (227 N. Prince St., 717/283-0940, www.senoritaburrita.net, café opens at 7:30 A.M. Mon.–Fri. and noon Sat., full menu available 11 A.M.–9 P.M. Mon.–Thurs., 11 A.M.–11 P.M. Fri., noon–11 P.M. Sat., $5–9) is just a couple of blocks away. California transplant Jennifer Foster opened the restaurant in 2003 (and the market stand in 2006) to sate her cravings for Mission-style burritos. Choose from specialty burritos such as the Mama Foster (rosemary olive oil tortilla, southwestern chicken, tomato basil rice, black beans, feta cheese, and more) or build your own with ingredients ranging from roasted red pepper hummus to vegan ground "beef" to grilled steak. The hip hangout also offers soups, salads, tacos, nachos, and more than half a dozen variations of rice and beans. Foster and staff grow many of the vegetables they use, buying the rest from local farms or Central Market's produce stands. The java comes from local roaster **Square One Coffee** (145 N. Duke St., 717/392-3354, www.squareonecoffee.com, 7 A.M.–11 P.M. Mon.–Fri., 9 A.M.–11 P.M. Sat.–Sun.), which deals exclusively in Fair Trade Certified and organically grown beans.

The Lancaster Dispensing Co. (33–35 N. Market St., 717/299-4602, www.dispensingco.com, kitchen 11 A.M.–midnight Mon.–Sat. and noon–9 P.M. Sun., bar open until 2 A.M. Mon.–Sat. and 10 P.M. Sun., $4–15) opened next to Central Market in 1978, before Lancaster had a restaurant scene to speak of. Designed with a Victorian pub in mind, DipCo offers a variety of salads, some south-of-the-border specialties, and hearty dinner entrées, but it's the overstuffed sandwiches that keep locals coming back. (The reasonable beer prices don't hurt.) Count on live music most Friday and Saturday nights.

Pick up a bottle of wine on your way to **Rachel's Cafe & Creperie** (309 N. Queen St., 717/399-3515, www.rachelscreperie.com, 7 A.M.–8 P.M. Tues.–Fri., 9 A.M.–8 P.M. Sat., 9 A.M.–3 P.M. Sun., $3–7), where the crepes are piping hot and the fillings inventive. The BYOB pays tribute to France with smoothie names like The Louvre, Monet's Garden, and Napoleon's Weakness but takes an international approach to crepe design. There's the pizza crepe and the Greek crepe, the veggie burrito crepe and the Thai chicken crepe, the smoked salmon crepe and the cheeseburger crepe. There's even a Philly cheese crepe (steak, American cheese, mushroom, scallions, and red onions). Building your own is always an option.

More upscale dining options abound. Lancaster County native Tim Carr lent his culinary talents to area country clubs before putting his name to a restaurant. Spitting distance from Central Market, **Carr's Restaurant** (50 W. Grant St., 717/299-7090, www.carrsres taurant.com, brunch 11:30 A.M.–2:30 P.M. Sun., lunch 11:30 A.M.–2:30 P.M. Tues.–Sat., dinner 5:30–9:30 P.M. Tues.–Thurs. and 5:30–10 P.M. Fri.–Sat., brunch $8–20, lunch $7–15, dinner $9–30) puts a sophisticated spin on comfort foods. There's no StarKist in the tuna noodle casserole, an artful presentation of thinly sliced rare tuna and wide noodles tossed with a rich butter sauce and wild mushrooms. The mac and cheese is loaded with Maine lobster chunks. Request a table near the back of the basement-level restaurant, where a glass wall affords a view of the wine cellar. You're welcome to bring your own bottle (a $15 corkage fee applies), but the Carr's selection is one of the best in town. In 2009 Carr opened **Crush Wine Bar** (4:30–9:30 P.M. Tues.–Thurs., 4:30–10 P.M. Fri.–Sat., noon–10 P.M. Sat.) above his restaurant. On offer: 20-odd wines by the glass and half glass, a carefully curated assortment of beers, several kinds of absinthe, and creative tapas ($6–11). Stop in if only to see what he means by Pennsylvania Dutch "sushi."

A short stroll away, German-born chef Gunter Backhaus presides over **The Loft** (201 W. Orange St., 717/299-0661, www.theloft lancaster.com, lunch 11:30 A.M.–2 P.M. Mon.–Fri., dinner 5:30–9 P.M. Mon.–Sat., lunch $9–14, dinner $16–34), locally famous for its jumbo shrimp cocktail. Backhaus doesn't shy away from the likes of frog legs, snails, and alligator tails—wait'll you see what the man can do with oysters—but timid palates needn't fear. The menu also features rosemary roasted free-range chicken, filet mignon, and lobster tails. Cozy and unpretentious, the restaurant gets its name from the open-beam ceiling in one of two dining rooms. The stems of potted plants cascade over the beams.

With a max capacity of 30 and a no-reservations policy, **Effie Ophelia** (230 N. Prince St., 717/397-6863, www.effieophelia.com, 5–10 P.M. Tues.–Sat., $22–30) might test your patience. But the wait is generally regarded as worth it, thanks to chef-owner Eric Howton's culinary artistry. An open kitchen allows patrons insight into the creative process. The curiously named BYOB doesn't accommodate parties larger than six.

It's not just dieters who sup on salad at the **Belvedere Inn** (402 N. Queen St., 717/394-2422, www.belvedereinn.biz, lunch 11 A.M.–2 P.M. Mon.–Fri., dinner 5–11 P.M. Sun.–Thurs. and 5 P.M.–midnight Fri.–Sat., bar open 11 A.M.–2 A.M. Mon.–Fri. and 5 P.M.–2 A.M. Sat.–Sun., lunch $7–14, dinner $12–32). The grilled Caesar salad at this elegant restaurant and bar is a thing of legend. Have it plain or choose from toppings including tenderloin tips, sautéed scallops, and grilled salmon. A petite version is available during the dinner hours, when entrées such as wild boar Bolognese and gnocchi with Maine lobster vie for attention. **Crazy Shirley's** (7 P.M.–2 A.M. Wed.–Thurs., 5 P.M.–2 A.M. Fri.–Sat.), a piano bar and lounge on the second floor of the Belvedere, hosts karaoke on Wednesdays, a DJ on Thursdays, and live jazz or blues on Fridays and Saturdays.

You might break into a song after a few sips of the Supercalifragilisticexpialidocious, a signature cocktail at **Checkers Bistro** (300 W. James St., 717/509-1069, www.checkersbistro .com, 11:30 A.M.–10 P.M. Tues.–Sat., bar open until 11 P.M., $8–32). It's a potent mix of vodka, gin, rum, triple sec, and banana liqueur, among other things. Supercalifragilisticexpialidocious is also an apt description for the contemporary restaurant near Lancaster's ballpark. Its small plates menu is particularly appealing, with options both common (chicken wings) and singular (Peking duck tacos). A breakfast menu available 11 A.M.–3 P.M. Saturdays is heavier on drinks than dishes. Wash down the brioche French toast with a Moon River White Sangria, a sparkling concoction of white wine, flavored brandy, and fresh fruit juices.

Like Checkers, **◖ FENZ Restaurant & Latenight** (398 Harrisburg Ave., Ste. 100, 717/735-6999, www.fenzrestaurant.com, dinner from 5 P.M. Mon.–Sat., lounge opens at 4 P.M., $14–28) excels in cocktails and small plates. Give the pickle fries a chance: the

Lancaster's FENZ Restaurant

tempura-battered kosher dill spears are positively addictive. Stylishly appointed with a clientele to match, FENZ has two levels with a bar on each. Have a look at both before settling in; the upstairs generally has a livelier, more youthful vibe. Take a seat at the downstairs bar to watch chef Daniella Ward at work. She's a whiz at vegetarian and vegan entrées. (The restaurant shares a 19th-century foundry building with a yoga studio, so she gets lots of practice.) Don't waste time searching for street parking. There's a lot behind the building, accessible from Charlotte Street.

A discussion of Lancaster's fine dining scene wouldn't be complete without words of praise for **Gibraltar** (931 Harrisburg Ave., 717/397-2790, www.kearesrestaurants.com/gibraltar, lunch 11:30 A.M.–2:30 P.M. Mon.–Fri., dinner 5–10 P.M. Mon.–Thurs., 5–10:30 P.M. Fri.–Sat., 4:30–9:30 P.M. Sun., bar open as late as 2 A.M., lunch $8–19, dinner $19–34), with its Mediterranean-influenced cuisine, *Wine Spectator*-lauded wine list, and gracious service. The seafood is simply phenomenal.

Start off with selections from the raw bar or an order of crab spring rolls and proceed to entrées like whole Adriatic Sea branzino (European seabass), rainbow trout stuffed with crab, and Moroccan spiced colossal shrimp. A tapas menu ($5–17) is available for those in the sharing spirit. Save room for one of pastry chef Anthony Valerio's confections.

Strasburg

Strasburg, with its train-related attractions and proximity to the Sight & Sound Theatres, sees large numbers of tourists. But its restaurants feel refreshingly un-touristy. Smack dab in the center of town, the **Strasburg Country Store & Creamery** (1 W. Main St., 717/687-0766, www.strasburg.com, 11 A.M.–10 P.M. Mon.–Sat., noon–10 P.M. Sun.) is best known as a destination for dessert and a dose of nostalgia. But it also offers soups, salads, sandwiches, and "Strasburgers" served with locally made potato chips. The house specialty is a bread bowl filled with PA Dutch–style chicken corn soup. As for dessert, choose from 20-plus flavors of ice

Strasburg Country Store & Creamery

cream and mix-ins such as M&Ms, raisins, and granola. Like the ice cream, the waffle cones are house-made, and the sweet aroma of sizzling batter hangs in the air. For a real indulgence, skip the cone and order an apple dumpling sundae. Ice cream isn't the only dessert option. A wide variety of chocolate-covered goodies vie for attention with fudge and peanut brittle, candy apples and caramel corn. Have a seat inside to soak in the old-timey touches, from vintage Cream of Wheat posters to a 19th-century marble soda fountain. Have a seat outside to watch horse-drawn buggies negotiating the intersection of Routes 741 and 896.

Purchased in 2003 by a husband and wife team with no experience in food service, **(The Iron Horse Inn** (135 E. Main St., 717/687-6362, www.ironhorsepa.com, noon–9 P.M. Mon. and Wed.–Thurs., noon–10 P.M. Fri.-Sat., noon–7 P.M. Sun., lunch $7–10, dinner $9–42) has emerged as one of those rare restaurants that pair fine food with a casual ambience. Denise Waller, one-half of the ownership

team and a nurse by training, buys broccoli, squash, potatoes, and other produce directly from local Amish farmers, shrinking the field-to-table timeline to a few hours in some cases. Lunch at the Iron Horse (a native American term for trains) can be as simple as a grilled ham and cheddar sandwich or as sophisticated as crepes stuffed with lump crabmeat. The asparagus fries—that's right: deep-fried spears of asparagus—go well with any dish. Dinner options range from an Angus beef burger to German/Austrian specialties to the triple steak, a marriage of portobello mushroom, Atlantic salmon, and succulent filet mignon. Chicken and waffles, served here more than a century ago when the building was known as The Hotel Strasburg, is available Sunday through Thursday. The lineup of draft beers features local brews along with German imports, and the wine list includes selections from Twin Brook Winery, about 10 miles east of Strasburg.

Just east of town on Route 741 is an outpost of regional chain **Isaac's Restaurant**

& Deli (226 Gap Rd., 717/687-7699, www .isaacsdeli.com, 10 A.M.–9 P.M. Mon.–Thurs., 10 A.M.–10 P.M. Fri.–Sat., 11 A.M.–9 P.M. Sun., call for winter hours, $6–12). The year was 1983 when two college buddies opened the first Isaac's in downtown Lancaster, and *Miami Vice* was soon to become a TV sensation. Hence the preponderance of pink flamingos in the bird-themed eateries scattered throughout south-central Pennsylvania. The Strasburg location, which shares an address with the Choo Choo Barn, a model railroader's mecca, boasts a dining area decked out like a train car. Its repertoire of made-from-scratch soups is 200 strong, but only the delicious creamy pepperjack tomato is available every day. The long list of sandwiches includes half a dozen veggie options. Pretzel sandwiches like the Salty Eagle (grilled ham, Swiss cheese, mustard) and Mallard (roast beef, bacon, mushrooms, melted cheddar, mild horseradish sauce) are particularly popular. Watching your carbs? Ask for a nest of romaine, mixed greens, or spinach in lieu of bread. You'll also find Isaac's in downtown Lancaster (25 N. Queen St., 717/394-5544), Lititz (4 Crosswinds Rd., 717/625-1181), and Ephrata (120 N. Reading Rd., 717/733-7777), among other places.

Lititz

The historic General Sutter Inn (14 E. Main St., 717/626-2115, www.generalsutterinn.com), located at the junction of Route 501 and East Main Street in the heart of Lititz, offers two restaurants along with 16 antique-filled guest rooms. The elegant **1764 Restaurant** (brunch 11 A.M.–3 P.M. Sun., lunch 11 A.M.–2:30 P.M. Mon.–Fri., 11 A.M.–3 P.M. Sat., dinner 5–9 P.M. Tues.–Thurs., 5–9:30 P.M. Fri.–Sat., 3–8 P.M. Sun., $7–30) isn't as pricey as its white tablecloths suggest. Its menu includes flatbread pizzas, burgers, and sandwiches for under $12 as well as loftier fare such as lobster and truffle mac and cheese and house-made basil gnocchi. The crab cakes sell like hotcakes. Alfresco dining is available Tuesdays through Sundays during the warmer months. The restaurant's name references the year the original inn was built.

(The current structure was built on the foundations of the original in the early 1800s.) In 2010 the inn unveiled a British-style pub, **Bulls Head Public House** (11:30 A.M.–4 P.M. Mon., 11:30 A.M.–10 P.M. Tues.–Thurs., 11:30 A.M.–10:30 P.M. Fri.–Sat., 11:30 A.M.–8 P.M. Sun., bar open until 11 P.M. Tues.–Thurs. and midnight Fri.–Sat., $5–15). Beer lovers are bonkers for the place, which boasts 14 rotating drafts and 80-plus bottles. The menu varies from day to day (check the chalkboard), but typical options include fish and chips, lamb shepherd's pie, chicken and leek pie, Scotch eggs, and mussels with blue cheese and bacon.

Columbia

Order the whoopee pie at ◖ **Prudhomme's Lost Cajun Kitchen** (50 Lancaster Ave., 717/684-1706, www.lostcajunkitchen.com, 4:30–11 P.M. Mon., 11 A.M.–11 P.M. Tues.–Thurs., 11 A.M.–midnight Fri.–Sat., 11 A.M.–8 P.M. Sun., $4–22) and what you'll get is a far cry from the classic Pennsylvania Dutch dessert. In place of the mound-shaped cakes: homemade cornbread. In place of the icing center: tender crabmeat. Served with a side of creamy mushroom sauce, the appetizer is a Lost Cajun original. Owners David and Sharon Prudhomme—he of Louisiana, she of New Jersey—brought their brand of Cajun cooking to Pennsylvania Dutch Country in 1992. The name Prudhomme should not be unfamiliar to foodies. David's uncle, Paul Prudhomme, owner of K-Paul's Louisiana Kitchen in New Orleans, is widely credited with popularizing Cajun cuisine. David learned the ropes in the restaurant his uncle opened in 1979. He makes just about everything from scratch—from salad dressings to the turkey andouille sausage that flavors his jambalaya—and still finds time to work the front of the house, where Sharon presides. Adventurous eaters delight in the menu, which includes turtle soup, alligator tail, and deep-fried bison testicles. But what Lost Cajun does best is blackened catfish. Try the melt-in-your-mouth catfish nuggets or the Cajun-meets-Mexican catfish fajita. The casual, playfully decorated restaurant and bar is also famous for its oversized onion rings. You'll need a knife and fork to attack these bad boys.

Mount Joy

Bube's Brewery (102 N. Market St., 717/653-2056, www.bubesbrewery.com) is reason enough to visit the town of Mount Joy, which at 14 miles northwest of Lancaster isn't particularly close to major tourist attractions. The one-of-a-kind Bube's is many things. For starters, it's a trip back in time. Listed in the National Register of Historic Places, the large brewery/restaurant complex looks much as it did in the late 1800s, when German immigrant Alois Bube produced lager beers there. Bube died in 1908, and the buildings were largely untouched until 1968, when restoration work began. Today they house a microbrewery, three restaurants, a store, and an art gallery. Occupying the original bottling plant is the **Bottling Works** (lunch served from 11 A.M. Mon.–Sat. and noon Sun., dinner served from 5 P.M. daily, $6–29), most casual of the restaurants. Its menu is typical of brewpubs: plenty of deep-fried munchies, soups and salads, burgers and sandwiches, and a selection of hearty entrées. Open-air dining is available in the adjacent **Biergarten,** where you'll find the huge boiler that created steam to power Mr. Bube's brewery. Reservations aren't required but are appreciated for groups of six or more.

It's best to make a reservation if you're keen on dining more than 40 feet below ground in the **Catacombs** (dinner served from 5:30 P.M. weekdays and 5 P.M. weekends, $24–39). The fine dining restaurant in the original brewery's stone-walled cellars offers the likes of roast duckling, crabmeat-stuffed lobster tail, and filet mignon amid candlelight. On most Sundays it serves a themed feast with a heaping side of theatrics. Bawdy medieval-themed feasts are most common, but its repertoire also includes Roman-, pirate-, and fairy-themed feasts, Halloween-themed feasts in October, and Christmas-themed feasts in December. Feast tickets must be purchased in advance.

Alois, the third restaurant, occupies the bar and dining rooms of the Victorian hotel Mr. Bube built onto his brewery. It hosts murder mystery dinners on Saturday nights throughout the year and several times a week around Halloween and Christmas. Tickets are $38 and should be purchased in advance.

Bube's Brewery merchandise is available in the **Cooper's Shed,** so called because it served as the original brewery's barrel-working shop. The store is open the same hours as the Catacombs. The **Brewery Gallery** (noon–9 P.M. daily and until 11 P.M. Fri.–Sun., free admission) changes exhibits monthly. The **Inn at Bube's Brewery** opened in 2010, offering rooms in the historic hotel at $100 per night.

INFORMATION

The **Pennsylvania Dutch Convention & Visitors Bureau** (717/299-8901, www.padutchcountry.com) is an excellent source of information about Lancaster County. Visit the website to request its free "getaway guide" or flip through a digital version. At the CVB's main visitors center (501 Greenfield Rd., Lancaster, 9 A.M.–6 P.M. Mon.–Sat. and 9 A.M.–4 P.M. Sun. Memorial Day weekend–Oct., 10 A.M.–4 P.M. daily Nov.–Memorial Day weekend), located just off U.S. 30 at the Greenfield Road exit, you can watch a brief film, load up on maps and brochures, and chat with travel consultants. One-hour tours of the Amish countryside ($20.95 per person, children 12 and under $10.95) depart from the visitors center at 10:30 A.M., noon, 1:30 P.M., and 3 P.M. daily from late May through October and select weekends in early May and November. The CVB also operates a visitors center in downtown Lancaster (1–3 W. King St., Lancaster, 717/299-6440, www.lancasterheritage.com, 9:30 A.M.–5 P.M. Mon.–Sat. and 10 A.M.–3 P.M. Sun. Memorial Day weekend–Oct., 10 A.M.–3 P.M. daily Nov.–Memorial Day weekend) in downtown Lancaster. For information about Pennsylvania Dutch Country as a whole, visit www.dutchcountryroads.com.

GETTING THERE AND AROUND

Lancaster County is about 90 minutes by car from Philadelphia and Baltimore. I-76 (Pennsylvania Turnpike) passes through the northern part of the county, but many of the main attractions lie along or near U.S. 30, which traverses the central part. Cape Air provides regularly scheduled flights between Baltimore/Washington International Thurgood Marshall Airport (BWI) and **Lancaster Airport** (717/569-1221, www.lancasterairport .com), six miles north of the city of Lancaster at the intersection of Route 501 (Lititz Pike) and Airport Road. Lancaster Airport's booking code is LNS. Rental cars are available at the airport. The larger Harrisburg International Airport (HIA) is about 30 miles from Lancaster.

Amtrak (800/872-7245, www.amtrak .com) provides rail service to the city. Bus service is available through **Greyhound** (800/231-2222, www.greyhound.com) and its interline partners. Trains and intercity buses pull into Lancaster Station (53 E. McGovern Ave.), built in 1929 by the Pennsylvania Railroad and now owned by Amtrak. It's about a mile north of downtown.

For getting around Lancaster County, it's best to have your own wheels, but public transportation is available. **Red Rose Transit Authority** (717/397-4246, www.red rosetransit.com) operates 17 bus routes, 11 of which serve Queen Street Station (225 N. Queen St., 717/393-3315, information center open 8 A.M.–5:30 P.M. Mon.–Fri. and 8 A.M.–4:30 P.M. Sat.–Sun.) in downtown Lancaster. The transit authority also operates the **Historic Downtown Trolley** on weekdays. (The trolley itself isn't historic. It's a thoroughly modern vehicle made to look like an old-time trolley.) Stops include Lancaster Station, a park-and-ride lot at Clipper Magazine Stadium, and Queen Street Station. One trolley trip is $1.50. An all-day pass costs $3.25.

Reading and Vicinity

With a population of roughly 80,000, Reading is the largest city in Pennsylvania Dutch Country. It was laid out in 1748 by sons of Pennsylvania founder William Penn and named the seat of Berks County several years later. By then the area was already home to an Amish community, one of the first in the country. Most Amish left Berks County in the latter part of the 1700s and early 1800s for reasons that may have included their pacifism. Reading was a military base during the French and Indian War, and its ironworks helped supply George Washington's troops with ammunition during the Revolutionary War. After Washington famously crossed the icy Delaware River in December 1776 and captured hundreds of Hessian soldiers garrisoned in Trenton, New Jersey, Reading hosted a prisoner-of-war camp.

The construction of the Reading Railroad in the 19th century ushered in the region's economic heyday. Built in the 1830s and '40s, the original mainline stretched south from the coal-mining town of Pottsville to Reading and then on to Philadelphia, a journey of less than 100 miles. Over the next century, the Reading grew into a many-tentacled transportation system with more than 1,000 miles of track. Heavily invested in Pennsylvania's anthracite coal industry, it reigned as one of the world's most prosperous corporations at the turn of the 20th century. Within a few decades, anthracite coal and rail transportation had both fallen out of favor. The railroad filed for bankruptcy and was absorbed by Conrail in the 1970s. But it lives on in the form of a property in the standard version of the board game Monopoly. One of Berks County's 30-plus historical museums and sites is dedicated to the railroad.

Historical attractions notwithstanding, the

the Reading Pagoda

county is best known as a shopping destination. It's home to an outlet mall and the only Cabela's outdoor megastore in Pennsylvania. It also has much to offer antiques lovers.

By the way, it's pronounced "RED-ing," not "REED-ing."

SIGHTS
The Pagoda

Reading's most prominent landmark is a building of the sort rarely seen outside the Far East. Perched atop Mount Penn, 886 feet above downtown, the Pagoda (Duryea Dr., 610/655-6271, www.readingpagoda.com, noon–5 P.M. Fri.–Sun. mid-June–Labor Day, noon–4 P.M. Sat.–Sun. rest of year, suggested donation $1) has become a symbol of the city. You'll see it in the logos of businesses and civic organizations and on a shoulder patch worn by the men and women of the Reading Police Department. More than a century old, it's believed to be one of only three pagodas of its scale in the country and the only one in the world with a fireplace and chimney. The story of how the multi-tiered tower came to be is as interesting as the structure

itself. "Reading to Have Japanese Pagoda," read a headline in the August 10, 1906, issue of the *Reading Eagle.* The man behind the plan was local businessman William Abbott Witman, who had made himself very unpopular by starting a stone quarrying operation on the western slope of Mount Penn. The Pagoda would cover the mess he'd left on the mountainside. Moreover, it would serve as a luxury resort.

The exotic building was completed in 1908, but Witman's plan to operate it as a mountain retreat was dealt a fatal blow: His application for a liquor license was denied. By 1910, the property was in foreclosure. To save the bank from a loss, local merchant and bank director Jonathan Mould purchased the Pagoda and presented it to the city as a gift. Before radios came into common use, the seven-story structure served as a sort of public announcement system. Lights installed on its roof flashed Morse code to direct firemen and relay baseball scores, political outcomes, and other information. Today the temple of stone and terracotta tiles is a popular tourist stop. Visitors can climb 87 solid oak steps to a lookout offering a view for 30-plus miles. There's a small café and gift shop on the first floor. The Pagoda is quite a sight at night, when it's aglow with red LED lights.

Reading Railroad Heritage Museum

Opened in 2008 in a former Pennsylvania Steel foundry complex, the Reading Railroad Heritage Museum (500 S. 3rd St., Hamburg, 610/562-5513, www.readingrailroad.org, 10 A.M.–4 P.M. Sat., noon–4 P.M. Sun., admission $5, seniors $4, children 5–12 $3) tells the story of the profound impact the railroad had on the communities it served. It's operated by the Reading Company Technical & Historical Society, which began rounding up locomotives and freight and passenger cars several years after the railroad's 1971 bankruptcy filing. The all-volunteer nonprofit is now the proud owner of the nation's largest collection of rolling stock dedicated to a single railroad. Tours of the outdoor display yard begin at 15 minutes past the hour, with the last scheduled at 2:15 P.M.

Reading Public Museum

The Reading Public Museum (500 Museum Rd., Reading, 610/371-5850, www.reading publicmuseum.org, 11 A.M.–5 P.M. Tues.–Thurs. and Sat., 11 A.M.–8 P.M. Fri., noon–5 P.M. Sun., admission $8, seniors, students, and children 4–17 $6) is part art museum, part natural history museum, and part anthropological museum. Founded in 1904 by a local teacher, the museum even has a gallery devoted to its own history. Its fine art collection is particularly strong in oil paintings and includes works by John Singer Sargent, Edgar Degas, Winslow Homer, N. C. Wyeth, George Bellows, Milton Avery, and Berks County native Keith Haring. Among the highlights of its natural history collection are the fossilized footprints of reptiles that roamed the immediate area some 200 million years ago. They were found just a few miles away. The anthropological and historical collections include everything from an Egyptian mummy to 16th-century samurai armor to Pennsylvania German folk art. As if that weren't enough, the museum boasts a 25-

acre arboretum and a full-dome planetarium. Admission to star shows, offered most Sunday afternoons, is $7 for adults and $5 for seniors, students, and children 4–17.

GoggleWorks Center for the Arts

Like other cities wrestling with the erosion of their industrial base, Reading has rolled out the red carpet for artists and cultural organizations. In 2005 an abandoned factory in Reading's urban core was transformed into the GoggleWorks Center for the Arts (201 Washington St., Reading, 610/374-4600, www.goggleworks.org, 9 A.M.–9 P.M. Mon.–Sat., 11 A.M.–7 P.M. Sun., free admission). So named because the factory manufactured safety goggles, the arts center boasts several galleries, a film theater, a café, dozens of artist studios, a wood shop, a ceramics studio, a jewelry studio, a glass-blowing facility, dance and music studios, and more. The GoggleWorks Store (10 A.M.–7 P.M. Mon.–Fri., 10 A.M.–6 P.M. Sat., 11 A.M.–5 P.M. Sun.) offers unique handcrafted items.

© GREATER READING CONVENTION & VISITORS BUREAU

glassblowing class at the GoggleWorks Center for the Arts

The best time to explore the six-building campus is during a **Second Sunday** open house, when most of the artists are in their studios. Held from 11 A.M.–4 P.M., the event features live music and walk-in workshops. The GoggleWorks and other venues in Reading's emerging arts district are also hopping on the **First Thursday** (www.penncorridor.com) evening of every month. The arts center is a good first stop on a visit to the area because it houses the Greater Reading Visitors Center, stocked with hundreds of brochures.

In 2008 **R/C Reading Movies 11** (30 N. 2nd St., 610/374-2828, www.rctheatres.com) opened a stone's throw from the GoggleWorks. The multiplex boasts Reading's first IMAX auditorium, stadium seating with high-back chairs, and a game room.

Boyertown Museum of Historic Vehicles

The Reading area is so associated with rail transportation that visitors are often surprised to learn of its role in automobile history.

Reading's Duryea Drive is named for Charles Duryea, who in the 1890s founded the first American company to manufacture and sell gasoline-powered vehicles. In 1900 the famous automaker moved from Massachusetts to Reading, in part because the railroad center had iron and steel foundries, machine shops, and skilled workers—everything needed for automobile manufacture. He stayed for 14 years, testing new vehicles on the steep, winding road that would bear his name. Duryea wasn't the only automaker to set up shop in Reading. Eleven companies manufactured automobiles in the city between 1900 and 1934. Most of the 50-odd cars, trucks, and motorcycles displayed at the Boyertown Museum (85 S. Walnut St., Boyertown, 610/367-2090, www.boyertownmuseum.org, 9:30 A.M.–4 P.M. Tues.–Sun., admission $6, seniors $5, students $4) were built in southeastern Pennsylvania. The collection also boasts rare examples of the horse-drawn vehicles that preceded them. It includes an 1875 fire cart hose made in a factory that operated on the site of the museum

Boyertown Museum

from 1872 to 1926 and trucks developed by the Boyertown Auto Body Works, which succeeded the carriage factory and remained in business until 1990. Located about 15 miles east of Reading, the museum hosts an annual antique and classic car show called **Duryea Day.** It's held on the Saturday of Labor Day weekend in Boyertown Community Park.

Before we leave the subject of cars, it should be mentioned that Duryea Drive, where so many early automobiles were tested, is the site of two annual races sponsored by the Pennsylvania Hillclimb Association (www.pahillclimb.org): the **Pagoda Hillclimb** in June and the longer **Duryea Hillclimb** in August.

◖ Air Museums

Berks County is home to not one but two museums dedicated to the history of aviation. Both offer thrill-of-a-lifetime rides in antique planes. Larger and older, the **Mid-Atlantic Air Museum (MAAM)** (11 Museum Dr., Reading, 610/372-7333, www.maam.org, 9:30 A.M.–4 P.M. daily, admission $6, children

6–12 $3) at Reading Regional Airport is home to more than 60 aircraft built from 1928 to the early 1980s. Among them is a Northrop P-61 Black Widow—one of only four in existence. In January 1945, the night fighter crashed into a mountainside on the South Pacific Island of New Guinea. World War II veteran Eugene "Pappy" Strine and his son established the air museum in 1980 for the purpose of recovering the rare aircraft, which had logged only 10 flight hours before stalling and crashing during a proficiency check. Green-lighted by the Indonesian government in 1984, the recovery project took seven years. The effort to restore it to flying condition was nearing completion in 2010. Other highlights of the collection include a North American B-25 Mitchell, a World War II bomber that appeared in half a dozen movies before she was donated to the museum in 1981, and a Douglas R4D-6 Skytrain, which delivered supplies and specialist personnel to combat zones during the war. MAAM's impressive holding of vintage military aircraft and annual **World War II Weekend** have given it a

Vintage warbirds take to the skies during World War II Weekend at the Mid-Atlantic Air Museum.

© PABLO SANCHEZ

reputation as a "warbird" museum, but in fact, about two-thirds of its flying machines were built for civilians.

Reading's airport was used as a military training airfield during World War II, and for three days each summer, it takes on the look and feel of that era. Held the first full weekend in June, WWII Weekend features air and military vehicle shows, battle re-creations, troop encampments, a militaria flea market, and 1940s entertainment, including big band dances. Single-day tickets are $20 in advance or $22 at the gate for adults, $9 in advance or $10 at the gate for children 6–12.

The **Golden Age Air Museum** (Grimes Airfield, 371 Airport Rd., Bethel, 717/933-9566, www.goldenageair.org, 10 A.M.–4 P.M. Sat. and 11 A.M.–4 P.M. Sun. May–Oct., year-round by appointment, admission $5, children 6–12 $3), about 20 miles away, was established in 1997. True to its name, it concentrates on the so-called golden age of aviation: the years between the two World Wars. More than 20 of its 30-some aircraft were built in the late 1910s, '20s, and '30s. The museum is also home to a handful of antique automobiles, including a

1930 Ford Model A roadster. Its **Flying Circus Air Shows,** held in June and August, pay tribute to barnstorming, a popular form of entertainment in the 1920s.

MAAM offers rides in a pair of 1940s aircraft, including an open-cockpit biplane trainer, on the second weekend of May and July–October, as well as during the WWII extravaganza. The cost of the flight, which lasts about 20 to 25 minutes, is $225. Reservations are required. Golden Age Air Museum offers rides in an open-cockpit 1929 biplane year-round by appointment. A 15-minute flight costs $99 for one person, $119 for two. One or two people can fly for 30 minutes for $199 or 60 minutes for $379.

Hopewell Furnace National Historic Site

If you ask a Pennsylvanian about the state's iron and steel heritage, he'll probably tell you about the fire-breathing plants that brought renown to cities such as Pittsburgh, Johnstown, and Bethlehem. Most people don't associate the industry with rural Pennsylvania. They haven't been to Hopewell Furnace National Historic

Hopewell Furnace National Historic Site

Site (2 Mark Bird Ln., Elverson, 610/582-8773, www.nps.gov/hofu, 9 A.M.–5 P.M. Wed.–Sun. and holidays including Memorial Day and Labor Day, restrooms and hiking trails open daily, free admission), which features the restored remains of an iron furnace and the village that grew around it. Established in 1771, Hopewell Furnace was one of dozens of "iron plantations" operating in southeastern Pennsylvania by the time the American colonies declared their independence from Great Britain. It supplied cannons, shot, and shells for patriot troops during the Revolutionary War. During the first half of the 19th century, the charcoal-fired furnace produced a wide variety of iron products, including pots, kettles, flatirons, and hammers, gaining fame for its stoves. Even Joseph Bonaparte, elder brother of Napoleon, ordered a Hopewell stove in 1822. After 112 years of operation, the outdated furnace closed in 1883. The workers and their families packed up and left.

Purchased by the federal government in 1935, the Hopewell Furnace property has been restored to the way it looked during its heyday in the 1830s and '40s. Visitors still have to use their imaginations: The National Park Service lacks the wizardry to recreate the billows of charcoal dust, noises, and stench that emanated from the active furnace. Exhibits in the visitors center and occasional living history programs help the imagination. The core of the Hopewell Furnace experience is strolling through the frozen-in-time village, popping into open buildings, so it's best to visit when the weather is nice. Early September through October is a particularly good time because the park's apple orchard, which includes historic varieties you won't find in the supermarket, is open for picking. The apples are sold by the pound. Hiking enthusiasts should plan to stay a while. More than 40 miles of trails traverse the 848-acre historic site and neighboring **French Creek State Park** (843 Park Rd., Elverson, 610/582-9680, www.dcnr.state.pa.us/stateparks/parks/frenchcreek.aspx).

◖ Hawk Mountain Sanctuary

Located 25 miles north of Reading, Hawk Mountain Sanctuary (1700 Hawk Mountain Rd., Kempton, 610/756-6000, www.hawkmountain.org, trails open dawn to dusk daily,

© HAWK MOUNTAIN SANCTUARY

one of several Hawk Mountain lookouts

HAVE A LAGER

If Pennsylvania had an official state beer, it would have to be **Yuengling Traditional Lager.** It's so ubiquitous and popular that asking for it by name is oftentimes unnecessary. Most bartenders translate "I'll have a lager" as "Pour me a Yuengling." Pronounced properly (YING-ling), the brand sounds like an import from the Far East. But the brewing company more properly known as D.G. Yuengling & Son has been based in Pottsville, Pennsylvania, since its 1829 founding. Yeah, about its age: Yuengling is America's oldest brewery, a fact

The Yuengling wagon delivers lager in the Memorial Day Parade in Summit Hill.

visitor center open 8 A.M.–5 P.M. daily Sept.–Nov., 9 A.M.–5 P.M. Dec.–Aug.) is one of the best places in the country to watch migrating hawks, eagles, falcons, and other winged predators. During the fall migration, counters may record upwards of 1,000 birds in one day. That's because of the sanctuary's location on the Blue Mountain (a.k.a. Kittatinny) ridge, part of the Appalachian range. In the fall, the topography and prevailing northwesterly winds conspire to create updrafts that allow raptors to glide, soar, and save energy on their southward journeys. Lookouts at Hawk Mountain allow for eye-level views of the majestic birds. Some fly so close that you can't help but duck. The migration begins in mid-August and continues

into December, peaking September through November. The very best time to visit is two or three days after a cold front passes. Sightings are considerably less frequent during the northbound migration, when prevailing easterlies push raptors west of the sanctuary. Still, it's possible to spot as many as 300 on a day in April or early May.

Founded in 1934 to stop hunters from shooting the migrants, Hawk Mountain is the world's oldest refuge for birds of prey. The nonprofit charges a fee for use of its eight-mile trail system, which connects to the epic Appalachian Trail. The fee is $5 for adults, $4 for seniors, and $3 for children 6–12 except on national holidays and weekends in September stamped on every bottle. It survived Prohibition by producing "near beers" – now known as non-alcoholic beers – and celebrated the 1933 repeal of the 18th Amendment by shipping a truckload of real beer to the White House. We don't know how then-president Franklin Roosevelt felt about the suds, but Barack Obama is a fan. When he lost a friendly wager on the outcome of the U.S.-Canada battle for ice hockey gold at the 2010 Winter Olympics, he sent a case of "lager" (as in Yuengling) to the Canadian prime minister.

About 35 miles north of Reading, Pottsville lies in Pennsylvania's coal region, home to the largest fields of anthracite in the country. The city is still recovering from the demise of the anthracite industry after World War II. Yuengling also had it rough in the post-war decades, as the full-flavored products of regional breweries lost favor to lighter national brands. But the company has more than recovered since Richard L. Yuengling Jr. became its fifth-generation owner in 1985. In 1999 it purchased a former Stroh brewery in Tampa, Florida, to keep up with demand. Two years later it opened a third brewery in Port Carbon, just a few minutes from Pottsville. By 2010 demand was again outstripping supply, necessitating an expansion of the newest plant. According to

a 2010 report by the Boulder, Colorado-based Brewers Association, Yuengling is the fourth largest brewing company in the country. Only Anheuser-Busch, MillerCoors, and Pabst sell more suds. Its rapid growth has much to do with the popularity of "lager," introduced in 1987. Yuengling produces half a dozen other beers but sells more lager than all the rest combined.

Free tours of the Pottsville brewery (5th and Mahantongo Streets, 570/628-4890, www.yuengling.com, gift shop open 9 A.M.-4 P.M. Mon.-Fri. year-round and 10 A.M.-3 P.M. Sat. Apr.-Dec.) are offered at 10 A.M. and 1:30 P.M. weekdays year-round and 11 A.M., noon, and 1 P.M. on Saturdays April through December. They include a visit to the "caves" where beer was fermented in years past, ending with free samples. You don't have to be of drinking age to take a tour, but you do have to wear closed shoes. Built in 1831, the facility isn't handicapped accessible.

While in Pottsville, you may want to pay a visit to **Jerry's Classic Cars and Collectibles Museum** (394 S. Center St., 570/628-2266, www.jerrysmuseum.com, noon-5 P.M. Fri.-Sun. May-Oct., admission $8), a tribute to the 1950s and '60s.

and November, when adults and seniors pay $7. The most popular path winds past a series of lookouts and is known, appropriately enough, as the Lookout Trail. The first lookout is only a couple hundred yards from the trailhead and is accessible by all-terrain wheelchair, available at the visitor center. The trail becomes rocky and uneven after the first few overlooks, but soldier on and you'll reap just rewards. At the end of the mile-long trail is the famed **North Lookout,** site of the sanctuary's official hawk count. It's hard to tear yourself away from the panoramic view from 1,490 feet above sea level, so consider bringing a cushion and something to eat or drink. Definitely pack food and water if you plan to tackle longer trails like the four-

mile River of Rocks loop, which drops into a valley and skirts an ice age boulder field. Trail maps are available on the sanctuary's website and in the visitor center.

If you're new to bird-watching, browse the visitor center's educational displays before starting your hike. A bit of time in the Wings of Wonder Gallery, featuring life-sized woodcarvings of each migrating raptor, will do wonders for your ability to identify the real deal. A pocket-sized guide to the various species that pass the sanctuary is available for purchase. You'll more than likely meet longtime visitors as you explore the sanctuary, many of whom can chirp up a storm about spotting and identifying birds. Educators are stationed at some lookouts during busy periods.

Hawk Mountain Line

Known as the Hawk Mountain Line because of its proximity to the bird sanctuary, the Wanamaker, Kempton & Southern (home station 42 Community Center Dr., Kempton, 610/756-6469, www.kemptontrain.com, regular ticket $8, children 3–11 $4) is a tourist railroad consisting of several miles of track purchased from the Reading Railroad in the 1960s and a collection of rolling stock that includes both steam and diesel-electric locomotives. The Reading began pulling up tracks in the 1970s, leaving the WK&S with two dead ends. Regular and themed train rides are offered on weekends April–December. Tickets for regular rides, which last about 40 minutes, can be purchased at the home station up to 10 minutes before departure. Reservations are required for murder mystery events, fall's "harvest moon" and haunted train rides, and December's Christmas-themed trips. The home station is off Route 737 in Kempton, an itty-bitty community about 30 miles north of Reading. From I-78, take exit 35 for Route 143 north or exit 40 for Route 737 north and continue about five miles to Kempton, where signs point the way to the station. Originally part of the vast Reading Railroad network, the station was moved from the southern tip of Berks County to its present location at the northern tip in 1963.

Crystal Cave Park

Discovered in 1871, Crystal Cave (963 Crystal Cave Rd., Kutztown, 610/683-6765, www.crystalcavepa.com, opens at 9 A.M. daily Mar.–Nov., closes between 5 and 7 P.M., admission $11.50, children 4–11 $7.50) is the oldest operating show cave in Pennsylvania. Guides who know their stalagmites from their stalactites lead visitors along concrete pathways, pointing out the "prairie dogs," the "totem pole," the "ear of corn," and other exquisite formations. Tours last 40 to 50 minutes and include a short video presentation on cave geology. It's a constant 54 degrees inside, so dress accordingly.

There's quite a bit to keep visitors entertained outside the cave, including an 18-hole miniature golf course ($4), a panning-for-gemstones attraction ($4.50 per gemstone bag), and an ice cream parlor and restaurant open daily in July and August and weekends in June and September. Amish buggy rides and use of the picnic facilities are included in the price of admission.

ENTERTAINMENT AND EVENTS
Concert Venues

Home to Reading's professional ice hockey and indoor football teams, the **Sovereign Center** (700 Penn St., Reading, 610/898-7469, tickets 800/745-3000, www.sovereigncenter.com, box office 10 A.M.–5 P.M. Mon.–Fri. year-round and 10 A.M.–2 P.M. Sat. Labor Day–Memorial Day) also hosts concerts, professional wrestling, conventions, and other events. Previous performers include Neil Diamond, Lynyrd Skynyrd, Kenny Chesney, Matchbox Twenty, Cher, Elton John, and Sting. Opened in 2001, the arena seats 7,000 for hockey matches and 8,900 for concerts. It's sometimes converted into a smaller, more intimate venue known as the **Reading Eagle Theater.**

Performing Arts

In 2000 the Berks County Convention Center Authority purchased Reading's only surviving movie palace, sank $7 million into renovations, and reopened it as the **Sovereign Performing Arts Center** (136 N. 6th St., Reading, 610/898-7469, tickets 800/745-3000, www.sovereigncenter.com, box office opens at noon on event days). The 1,700-seat theater is home to the **Reading Symphony Orchestra** (www.readingsymphony.org), founded in 1913, and **Reading Civic Theatre** (www.readingcivic.org), which began staging musicals one year later. It also hosts touring Broadway productions, popular music concerts, and other events.

The **Miller Center for the Arts** (4 N. 2nd St., Reading, 610/372-4721 ext. 5500, www.racc.edu/MillerCenter) also welcomes a wide array of touring acts—from modern dance to classical marionette theater. The glass-walled theater on the campus of Reading Area Community College opened in 2007. It seats about 500.

Festivals and Events

First held in 1991, **Berks Jazz Fest** (various venues, tickets 800/745-3000, www.berksjazzfest.com, Mar.) has grown bigger and bigger over the years. Famed trumpeter Wynton Marsalis, who played at the inaugural fest, returned in 2010 with his Jazz at Lincoln Center Orchestra. Other past performers include Eliane Elias, the Dirty Dozen Brass Band, John Tesh, Béla Fleck and the Flecktones, David Sanborn, the Count Basie Orchestra, Buddy Guy, Susan Tedeschi, and Kurt Elling. The 10-day festival is presented by the Berks Arts Council, which is also to thank for a series of free concerts held on Friday evenings in the summer. The **Bandshell Concerts** (City Park, 1261 Hill Rd., Reading, 610/898-1930, www.berksarts.org) showcase various musical genres, including blues, doowop, and bluegrass.

Berks County's premier event is the **Kutztown Folk Festival** (Kutztown Fairgrounds, 225 N. White Oak St., Kutztown, 888/674-6136, www.kutztownfestival.com, late June/early July, admission charged, free for children 12 and under), a nine-day celebration of Pennsylvania Dutch culture. Founded in 1950, it's said to be the oldest continuously operated folklife festival in the country. To call it a unique event is an understatement. Where else can you see a reenactment of a 19th-century hanging, watch a Mennonite wedding, take a seminar on the PA Dutch dialect, *and* buy bread baked in an early 1800s oven? The festival also features one of the largest quilt sales in the country. More than 2,500 locally handmade quilts are available for purchase; collectors from around the world attend an auction of the prize-winners. Demonstrations of quilting and other traditional crafts are a hallmark of the event. The words "Pennsylvania Dutch" are practically synonymous with "pig-out," and the Kutztown extravaganza does nothing to dispel that association. All-you-can-eat ham and chicken dinners are a festival tradition, as is roasting a 1,200-pound ox over a bed of coals. The borough of Kutztown is about 20 miles northeast of Reading.

Folks who like it hot descend on an itty-bitty community four miles south of Kutztown for the **Chili Pepper Food Festival** (William Delong Park, 233 Bowers Rd., Bowers, www.pepperfestival.com, Sept., admission by donation). The two-day event features a jalapeno-eating contest, a salsa contest, and even a chili pepper song contest. Excursions to a local chili pepper field are offered both days.

Winter's main event is a Christmas display on steroids. **Koziar's Christmas Village** (782 Christmas Village Rd., Bernville, 610/488-1110, www.koziarschristmasvillage.com, first weekend of Nov. to first weekend of Jan., admission charged) traces its history to 1948, when William M. Koziar strung lights around his house and barn in rural Berks County to the delight of his wife and four children. Each year, he stepped up his game, decorating more and more of his property. The increasingly elaborate display began attracting people from nearby and then people from not-so-nearby. These days more than half a million Christmas lights go into the creation of the winter wonderland. A reflective lake doubles the wow factor. There's more to Koziar's than twinkling lights. It also offers large dioramas of scenes such as "Christmas Beneath the Sea" and "Santa's Post Office," extensive model train layouts, and shops selling ornaments, souvenirs, toys, and other gifts. Santa's on site, of course.

SHOPPING
VF Outlet Center

One of greater Reading's most popular tourist destinations, the VF Outlet Center (801 Hill Ave., Wyomissing, 610/378-0408, www.vfoutletcenter.com, 9:30 A.M.–7 P.M. Mon.–Thurs., 9:30 A.M.–9 P.M. Fri.–Sat., 10 A.M.–5 P.M. Sun. Jan.–Feb., 9:30 A.M.–9 P.M. Mon.–Sat., 10 A.M.–6 P.M. Sun. Mar.–Dec.) has about 50 stores and a rich history. For most of the 20th century, its buildings comprised the Berkshire Knitting Mills. The Berkie, as locals called it, was the world's largest manufacturer of hosiery in the early decades of the century, before seamless nylons became all the rage. In 1969 it was purchased by VF Corporation, which opened a factory store in one end of a manufacturing building. A drop cloth separated the retail and manufacturing areas. The mill ceased operations several years later, but the store remained. Today the VF Outlet store is stocked with brands including Wrangler, Lee, JanSport, and Nautica. Other stores in the mill-turned-mall include Tommy Hilfiger, Liz Claiborne, Timberland, Reebok, OshKosh B'gosh, Black & Decker, and Dooney & Bourke.

Cabela's

The 2003 opening of a Cabela's store less than 20 miles north of Reading warranted a story in *The New York Times* travel section. After all, it was the first Cabela's outpost on the East Coast. The revered retailer of outdoor gear has since expanded into Connecticut and Maine, but the Pennsylvania store (100 Cabela Dr., Hamburg, 610/929-7000, www.cabelas.com, 8 A.M.–9 P.M. Mon.–Sat., 9 A.M.–8 P.M. Sun., call for winter hours) still reels in millions of hunting and fishing enthusiasts a year. The 250,000-square-foot showplace just off I-78 features shooting and archery ranges, massive aquariums, life-sized wildlife dioramas that put many natural history museums to shame, and a restaurant offering sandwiches stuffed with your choice of meats—the choices including elk, wild boar, bison, and ostrich. And then there's the merchandise. The dizzying selection includes everything from guns to outdoor-inspired home decor. Live bait is available for anglers heading to nearby waters. Also available: kennels for shoppers who bring their canine friends, a corral for those who bring their equine friends, and a dump station for those arriving by RV.

Antiques

Antiques lovers can find plenty of what they're looking for in the Reading area. Just 10 miles southwest of Reading, straddling Berks and Lancaster Counties, is the borough of Adamstown, also known as "Antiques Capital USA." See the *Lancaster County* section for the lowdown on Adamstown. Twenty miles

northeast of Reading is another antiquing destination: Kutztown's **Renninger's Antiques Market** (740 Noble St., Kutztown, 570/385-0104 Mon.–Thurs., 610/683-6848 Fri.–Sat., www.renningers.com, indoor antiques market 8 A.M.–4 P.M. Sat.). With locations in Adamstown and Florida as well as Kutztown, Renninger's is a big name in antiquing circles. The Kutztown market is open Saturdays and the Adamstown market Sundays, so it's not unusual for treasure hunters to hit both in one weekend. Kutztown's Renninger's began as a farmers market in 1955. Antiques dealers have been setting up shop since 1974. These days you'll find 200 booths in the indoor antiques market and as many as 100 more in the flea market outside. The flea market opens at 7 A.M., an hour before the indoor market. Thanks to large pavilions, it operates even during the winter months. What's for sale? Everything from Indian artifacts and early farm tools to neon beer signs and Pez dispensers.

Three times a year, hundreds of dealers from around the country descend on the grounds for an **Antiques & Collectors Extravaganza** (last full Thurs.–Sat. of Apr., June, and Sept., admission charged). Renninger's Kutztown also hosts a biannual antique radio show. It hasn't forgotten its roots as a farmers market. Open 10 A.M.–7 P.M. Fridays and 8 A.M.–4 P.M. Saturdays year-round, the indoor **Renninger's Farmers Market** has a strong Pennsylvania Dutch flavor. You'll find produce, fresh and smoked meats, baked goods, handmade candies, gourmet coffees and teas, and french fries to die for.

SPORTS AND RECREATION
Spectator Sports

The Reading area boasts minor league baseball, hockey, and soccer franchises, a professional indoor football team, and a drag racing track good for adrenaline-pumping entertainment eight months of the year. The **Reading Phillies** (FirstEnergy Stadium, 1900 Centre Ave., Reading, 610/370-2255, www.reading phillies.com) have been the AA affiliate of the Philadelphia Phillies since 1967. Only one

Minor League Baseball team has had a longer relationship with its parent club. The R-Phils, as they're known, have a devoted following, attracting more fans than any other team in the Eastern League year after year. It doesn't hurt that FirstEnergy Stadium is a classic beauty. Completed in 1951, the ballpark has undergone a series of renovations and additions since the late 1980s. The most ambitious was the construction of a 1,000-square-foot pool behind the right field fence. Game day tickets to the pool pavilion, which boasts a picnic area with TVs on each table, are $23–27 and include an all-you-can-eat buffet complete with barbecued ribs and corn on the cob.

Founded in 2001, Reading's ECHL ice hockey team has yet to bring home a championship. But the **Reading Royals** (Sovereign Center, 7th and Penn Streets, Reading, 610/898-7825, www.royalshockey.com) have produced more than a dozen National Hockey League players, including Los Angeles Kings goaltender Jon Quick, who earned a spot on the U.S. team for the 2010 Olympics. The Royals are affiliated with the NHL's Toronto Maple Leafs and Boston Bruins and the American Hockey League's Toronto Marlies. They share an arena with the **Reading Express** (800/745-3000, www.expressindoorfootball.com), a professional indoor football team that began play in 2006.

On the eve of its 2010 inaugural season, Major League Soccer's Philadelphia Union announced an affiliation with Reading's minor league franchise. Formed 15 years earlier as the alliteratively pleasing Reading Rage, the team was rebranded as **Reading United A.C.** (Exeter Township Senior High School, 201 E. 37th St., Reading, 610/927-4474, www.readingunitedac.com). It competes in the United Soccer Leagues' Premier Development League, considered the fourth tier of competition in North America.

Older than any of the minor league teams, **Maple Grove Raceway** (30 Stauffer Park Ln., Mohnton, 610/856-9200, www.maplegroveraceway.com) has been the site of many firsts in drag racing history. Best known as home

of the annual NHRA (National Hot Rod Association) Toyo Tires Nationals, the quarter-mile strip about 10 miles south of Reading hosts a wide variety of auto-centric events on weekends from March to November. It's best not to blink when jet-powered vehicles take to the track. Opened in 1962, Maple Grove also hosts a spring, summer, and fall flea market.

ACCOMMODATIONS
Reading

Though it's the cultural, governmental, and business capital of Berks County, downtown Reading has few lodging options. Its only hotel is the historic **◖ Abraham Lincoln** (100 N. 5th St., 610/372-3700, www.wyndhamreadinghotel.com, $99–159), a Wyndham property since 2005. Conveniently located within three blocks of the GoggleWorks Center for the Arts, the Sovereign Center, and the Sovereign Performing Arts Center, the hotel offers 104 rooms and 32 suites, two restaurants, a 24-hour gift shop, and free shuttle service to area businesses and attractions. Abraham Lincoln never slept here. The hotel, which opened in 1930, is named for the nation's 16th president because his great-grandfather lived nearby. Music fans and Marines will be interested to know that John Philip Sousa, the famed composer of military marches, suffered a heart attack while rehearsing in the area in 1932 and died in his 14th floor room at the Abraham Lincoln. With its original chandeliers, stately pillars, and brass and wrought iron railings, the hotel lobby is worth a peek even if you're just passing by.

The great stone mansion now known as the **Stirling Guest Hotel** (1120 Centre Ave., 610/373-1522, www.stirlingguesthotel.net, $150–300) was built in the early 1890s in what was then considered a far suburb of Reading. It's a mere mile north of the city center. Designed in the Châteauesque style for a local iron and steel magnate and named for a castle in Scotland, the mansion has nine sumptuously decorated guest suites. A large Tudor-style carriage house offers six more.

Less than a mile north of the VF Outlet

Center, **The Inn at Reading** (1040 N. Park Rd., Wyomissing, 610/372-7811, www.innat reading.com, $95–149) has 170 traditionally furnished rooms and suites. Amenities include a large outdoor pool open May through September, a half-court basketball court, an exercise facility, and a restaurant modeled on a traditional English pub. Breakfast is on the house Monday–Friday.

Northern Berks County

Pheasants, quail, and chukar, oh my! **Wing Pointe** (1414 Moselem Springs Rd., Hamburg, 610/562-6962, www.wingpt.com) is a resort custom-made for sport-shooting enthusiasts. From September through March, shotgun-toting guests hunt game birds released onto the grounds. Rental dogs and guides are available. The resort 15 minutes from outdoor megastore Cabela's also offers skeet and sporting clays shooting. Its main lodge features four guest suites ($145–191), a common room with a fireplace and large-screen TV, and an outdoor pool and whirlpool. Parties of up to nine people can rent a five-bedroom retreat ($550 for four guests, $83 per additional guest) with plush furnishings, a large modern kitchen, a formal dining room, and its own pool and whirlpool.

For those who venture to these parts to aim binoculars rather than shotguns at birds, there's ◖ **Pamela's Forget Me Not B&B** (33 Hawk Mountain Rd., Kempton, 610/756-3398, www.pamelasforgetmenot.com, $99–159). A short drive from the famed Hawk Mountain Sanctuary and the Appalachian Trail, the B&B is as charming as its name. It offers three suites complete with Jacuzzis and one room with a shared bath. Made for romance, the Cottage Suite features a hand-crafted four-poster bed, gas fireplace, and private deck. (The couple that purchased the B&B in 2006 stayed here as guests on the night of their 1999 engagement.) The comfy Carriage House Suite, which sleeps up to six people, is perfect for families. The remaining suite and guest room are in the main house, dating to 1879 and Victorian in decor.

FOOD
Reading

Most of Reading's recommendable restaurants are concentrated in the gritty downtown area. The most famous, thanks to its longevity and a 2008 visit from the Travel Channel, is **Jimmie Kramer's Peanut Bar** (332 Penn St., 610/376-8500, www.peanutbar.com, 11 A.M.–11 P.M. Mon.–Thurs., 11 A.M.–midnight Fri., noon–midnight Sat., $7–25). At the "bar food paradise," as the Travel Channel dubbed it, patrons are welcomed with a bowl of peanuts and encouraged to toss the shells on the floor. The casual joint is also known for its hot wings, seafood, house-made desserts, and draft beer blends. Opened in 1933 as Jimmie Kramer's Olde Central Cafe, the bar and restaurant originally plied patrons with pretzels. When the pretzels ran out one day in 1935, Jimmie sent someone to a peanut roaster across the street, and the shell-tossing tradition was born. Renamed for the humble legume in 1958, the restaurant is now run by Jimmie's grandson.

One block south of the Peanut Bar is a cluster of three restaurants owned by local chef Judy Henry. **Judy's on Cherry** (332 Cherry St., 610/374-8511, www.judysoncherry.com, open for lunch Tues.–Fri. and dinner Tues.–Sat., lunch $8–14, dinner $9–30), a self-described "hearth-fired Euro café," offers Mediterranean-style fare. The lunch menu features salads, sandwiches, and pasta dishes. Dinnertime selections include the likes of pan-seared golden sea bass and half rack of lamb. Elegant small plates and crispy thin-crusted pizzas are always on offer, and warm focaccia sprinkled with sea salt is free with every meal. The adjoining **Speckled Hen Cottage Pub & Alehouse** (30 S. 4th St., 610/685-8511, www .speckledhenpub.com, 4:30 P.M.–midnight Wed.–Thurs. and 4:30 P.M.–1 A.M. Fri.–Sat. Oct.–Apr., $8–19) offers an altogether different dining experience. Henry transformed downtown Reading's oldest building—a log house built in the 1780s—into the sort of pub you'd find in the countryside of England or Ireland. With its working fireplaces and comfort cuisine (shepherd's pie, bangers and mashed potatoes, meatloaf, beef pot roast, baked mac and cheese, and such), the Speckled Hen hits the spot on a wintry day. Come spring, Henry closes it and opens **Plein Air** (lunch 11:30 A.M.–2 P.M. Wed.–Fri., dinner 5–10 P.M. Wed.–Sat., open mid-May–Sept., $8–18), an outdoor café accessible from either Judy's or the Speckled Hen. The fare is light and summery and the featured cocktail a tangerine mojito with fresh mint.

For margaritas in more than half a dozen flavors, head to **Mezcal's** (150 N. 6th St., 610/685-5272, www.dineindie.com/mezcals, 11 A.M.–3 P.M. Mon., 11 A.M.–8 P.M. Tues.–Thurs., 11 A.M.–9 P.M. Fri.–Sat., noon–8 P.M. Sun., lunch under $10, dinner $7–17). Set in a typical Reading row house, the colorful Mexican eatery offers a lengthy menu and a laid-back vibe.

Downtown's chicest dining establishment is also tucked inside a row house. **Dans Restaurant** (1049 Penn St., 610/373-2075, 5–9:30 P.M. Wed.–Sat., noon–7 P.M. Sun., dinner $19–36, Sun. brunch $7–29) is no longer owned by the two Dans who opened it in 1989 but carries on their mission of providing "a contemporary alternative to the traditional Berks County dining scene." Its French-influenced dinner menu changes weekly. The Sunday brunch, served noon–3 P.M., is the best in town. Choose from such dishes as fried duck eggs, griddle cakes with Ghirardelli white chocolate, and brie and tomato fondue omelet, or splurge on the five-course tasting menu ($29). Dans is quite small, and reservations are very much recommended.

Just outside the downtown area is the lovely **Abigail's Tea Room** (1441 Perkiomen Ave., 610/376-6050, www.abigailstearoom.com, seating 11 A.M.–3 P.M. Wed.–Sat.), which offers a simple lunch menu ($6–9) as well as afternoon tea experiences ($17–20). For the latter, be sure to make a reservation at least a day in advance. Abigail's is Victorian through and through, from its setting—an 1883 manse outfitted with period furnishings and crystal chandeliers—to its delicate floral china. You wouldn't look a bit out of place in a wide-brimmed, feather-trimmed hat. There's a tea-centric gift shop on site, and guess what: Lady Gaga has been photographed with exquisite teacups purchased from the owner's website.

Northern Berks County

With a name like **Deitsch Eck** (87 Penn St., Lenhartsville, 610/562-8520, www.deitscheck .com, 4–8 P.M. Wed.–Thurs., 4–9 P.M. Fri.–Sat., 11:30 A.M.–7 P.M. Sun., $4–15), it has to be Pennsylvania Dutch. Chef-owner Steve Stetzler began working in the corner restaurant (Deitsch Eck means "Dutch Corner") when he was 15 and bought it nine years later in 1997. His mother and sister are among the staff. In addition to heaping portions of PA Dutch cooking, they serve a wide variety of burgers and sandwiches and Italian favorites like veal parmigiana. A meat market in their quaint country town provides the ground beef, hams, pork chops, and sausages.

INFORMATION AND SERVICES

The **Greater Reading Convention & Visitors Bureau** (610/375-4085, www.readingberks pa.com) is a good source of information about the area. Visit the website to request a free copy of its official visitors guide or peruse a digital version. The guide and some 300 brochures are available at the CVB's visitors center in the **GoggleWorks Center for the Arts** (201 Washington St., Reading, 9 A.M.–9 P.M. Mon.–Sat., 11 A.M.–7 P.M. Sun.). For information about Pennsylvania Dutch Country as a whole, visit www.dutchcountryroads.com.

GETTING THERE AND AROUND

Located about 60 miles northeast of Philadelphia and 30 miles northwest of Lancaster, Reading is primarily a drive-to destination. It's accessible by I-78, I-76 (Pennsylvania Turnpike), U.S. 222, and U.S. 422. There hasn't been scheduled service to Reading Regional Airport, home to the Mid-Atlantic Air Museum, for several years. Lehigh Valley International Airport (ABE), served by airlines including Delta, United, and AirTran, is 40 miles from Reading. Harrisburg

International Airport (HIA) and Philadelphia International Airport (PHL) are about 60 miles away. **Schuylkill Valley Airport Shuttle** (610/929-1775, www.svairportshuttle.com) provides van service between Reading Regional and Philadelphia International. The one-way fare is $50 for one adult, $80 for two, and $100 for three. Reservations are required.

Intercity bus service to Reading is available through **Greyhound** (800/231-2222, www.greyhound.com) and its interline partners. Local bus service is provided by the Berks Area Reading Transportation Authority, or **BARTA** (610/921-0601, www.bartabus.com). Call **Reading Metro Taxi** (610/374-5111) if you need a lift.

Hershey and Vicinity

Hershey is a town built on chocolate as surely as if cocoa were used in place of concrete. It owes its name and existence to Milton S. Hershey, founder of the largest chocolate company in North America. Milton Hershey was born in 1857 in a small central Pennsylvania community. His family moved frequently while his father pursued a series of get-rich schemes, and as a consequence, he never advanced past the fourth grade. At 14, he began a four-year apprenticeship with a Lancaster confectioner—and found his calling. But the young candy maker wasn't immediately successful. His first

candy business, in Philadelphia, collapsed after six years. In 1883 he opened a candy shop in New York. Again, his venture failed. Penniless, he returned to Lancaster and gave it a third try, making caramels by day and selling them from a pushcart in the evenings. A large order from a British candy importer and a loan from a local bank marked a turning point for the persistent entrepreneur. His Lancaster Caramel Company soon became one of the leading caramel manufacturers in the country, and he became a very rich man.

At the Chicago World's Fair in 1893,

Hershey is called "The Sweetest Place on Earth."

© RICHARD BITTING

Hershey was transfixed by an exhibit of German chocolate-making equipment. He purchased the machinery and had it installed in the east wing of his caramel factory. The Hershey Chocolate Company was born.

Back then, milk chocolate was a Swiss luxury product. Hershey was determined to develop a formula for affordable milk chocolate, and by the dawn of the new century, he had succeeded. He sold the Lancaster Caramel Company for $1 million, retaining his chocolate-making machinery, and in 1903 broke ground on a new, larger factory. The site: a cornfield in Derry Township, Pennsylvania, about a mile from his birthplace. It wasn't simply nostalgia that brought him back. Hershey needed fresh milk for his milk chocolate, and the area was rich in dairy farms. There was a railroad line and turnpike nearby. The absence of housing and other infrastructure for future employees didn't faze Hershey. He was bent on building not only a manufacturing plant but also a model town.

The intersection of two dirt roads a short distance from the factory became the center of his town. He named one Chocolate Avenue and the other Cocoa Avenue. A trolley system was up and running even before the factory was completed. As Americans fell in love with Hershey's chocolate, homes for workers and executives were built on streets named after cocoa-growing regions: Trinidad, Java, Ceylon, and such. Hershey saw to it that builders used a variety of designs so that the community wouldn't look like a company town. It wasn't long before his eponymous town had a fire company, barber shop, blacksmith shop, gas station, service garage, and weekly newspaper. He had set aside land for a park, and by 1910 it boasted a band shell, swimming pool, zoo, and bowling alley. Today Hersheypark boasts 11 roller coasters and dozens of other rides. Sales of Hershey's chocolates grew even during the Great Depression, and so did the town. Taking advantage of low-cost materials, the chocolate magnate launched a massive building campaign that employed hundreds of people. Among the town's Depression-era landmarks are the

© KATE HOPKINS

The street lights in Hershey are shaped like Hershey's Kisses.

grand Hotel Hershey and Hersheypark Arena, home to the Hershey Bears hockey team (originally named the Hershey B'ars) until 2002 and site of a massive surprise party on Milton Hershey's 80th birthday. He died in 1945 at the age of 88.

The Hershey Company, as it's now named, does business all over the world. It has plants in places as far-flung as Brazil and Mexico. But the company founded by Milton Hershey is still based in the town built by Milton Hershey—a town with streetlights shaped like Hershey's Kisses. It still makes chocolate there. You can smell it in the air. "The Sweetest Place on Earth," as Hershey is called, attracts several million visitors a year. Factory tours are no longer given, but it's still possible to learn a world about chocolate and the man who brought it to the masses. Start at the town's newest attraction, The Hershey Story, The Museum on Chocolate Avenue, for an excellent overview. Of course, if you have kids in tow, as a great deal of visitors do, they'll probably insist on starting at Hersheypark. Wherever you start, pace yourself. This place is right up there with Disney World in its concentration of attractions.

SIGHTS
◖ The Hershey Story

The Hershey Story (63 W. Chocolate Ave., Hershey, 717/534-3439, www.hersheystory .org, opens at 9 A.M. daily, closing time varies) opened in 2009, the first new landmark building on Chocolate Avenue in 75 years. It delivers exactly what its name promises: the story of the man, the company, and the town named Hershey. The story unfolds on the museum's second floor, where visitors learn about Milton Hershey's childhood and rocky road to success, his chocolate-making innovations and creative promotion strategies, his model town, and his philanthropies. Among the artifacts displayed are a chocolate-mixing machine from the 1920s and a Hershey's Kisses–wrapping machine, both in working order. Admission to the exhibit area is $10 for adults, $9 for seniors, $7.50 for children 3–12.

The main floor features the Chocolate Lab, where kids and adults can get hands-on experience in chocolate-making. Arrive early if you're interested. Classes can only be booked on the day of, and they fill quickly. They're $10 for adults, $9 for seniors, $7.50 for children 4–12. Children under 4 aren't permitted in the lab. Combo tickets are available for visitors who want to take in the exhibits and take part in a class: $17.50 for adults, $16.50 for seniors, $14 for children.

Also on the main floor is Café Zooka, named after one of Milton Hershey's early chocolate novelties. You won't find his Chocolate Zooka Sticks on the menu (they were discontinued in 1904), but you will find a variety of sandwiches, salads, pizzas, and desserts. Leave room for the Countries of Origin Chocolate Tasting, located within the café. You can sample six warm drinking chocolates, each representing a different chocolate-growing region, for $9.95.

Even before his chocolate factory was built, Milton Hershey had laid out the plans for a town. He'd set aside 150 acres along Spring

The Hershey Story describes the history of the Hershey legacy.

© THE HERSHEY STORY

Hersheypark

Creek for a park where his employees could picnic and paddle the day away. The park opened in the spring of 1907 and soon became a tourist attraction, with excursion trains and trolleys delivering fun-seekers from surrounding communities.

◖ Hersheypark

Today Hersheypark (100 W. Hersheypark Dr., Hershey, 717/534-3900, www.hersheypark .com) lures people from across the state and beyond with more than 60 rides and attractions, including 11 roller coasters. The historic park spends generously to stay current. Four of the coasters were installed in the 21st century, including Lightning Racer, the first wooden dueling coaster in the U.S. The newest coaster, Fahrenheit, features trains with stadium-style seating and a 97-degree drop. Bring bathing suits to enjoy Hersheypark's water attractions, which include Tidal Force, one of the tallest splash-down rides in the world; Roller Soaker, an aerial ride that pits riders against spectators armed with water sprayers; and a series of tubing rides. A huge wave pool and 1,300-foot lazy river were added in 2009. For those who prefer to stay firmly planted on the earth, Hersheypark offers shopping and a busy schedule of live entertainment.

The park is open weekends in May, daily from late May through Labor Day, and a few weekends after Labor Day. Gates open at 10 A.M. and close between 6 P.M. and 11 P.M. A variety of admission plans are available. One-day admission is $52.95 for guests ages 9–54, $31.95 for children 3–8 and adults 55–69, $20.95 for those 70 and older. Hang on to your ticket stub in case you decide to come back the next day; consecutive-day admission is $31.95. Arrive within a few hours of closing for special "sunset" rates. Flex passes, good for admission to the park on any two or three days of the season, are available. If your summer plans also include a visit to Dutch Wonderland in Lancaster, part of the Hershey family of attractions, ask about combo tickets. Hersheypark tickets are good for same-day admission to ZooAmerica.

The park opens on select weekends outside of its regular season. **Springtime in the Park** (www.springtimeinhershey.com) is a chance to preview what's in store for summer over several days in April. **Hersheypark in the Dark** (www .halloweeninhershey.com) is several weekends' worth of Halloween-themed fun. The park is also open in late November and throughout December for **Christmas in Hershey** (www .christmasinhershey.com). Meet Santa's

reindeer and take in a light show set to holiday tunes at Hersheypark. Then hop in the car and crank up the heater for Hershey Sweet Lights, a drive-thru spectacular located a few minutes from the amusement park.

ZooAmerica

In 1905, a couple from Lebanon, Pennsylvania, approached Milton Hershey with an idea. Several years earlier they'd immigrated from Germany, where they'd owned 12 prairie dogs and a bear cub. Alas, their yard in Lebanon couldn't accommodate their brood. They figured Hershey's proposed park could. ZooAmerica (30 Park Ave., Hershey, 717/534-3900, www.zooamerica.com, open year-round, hours vary, admission $9.50, children 3–8 and seniors $8, free admission with Hersheypark ticket) traces its history to their meeting with the chocolate magnate. The 11-acre zoo is home to more than 200 animals from five regions of North America. Visitors are never terribly far from the critters but have a rare opportunity to get even closer on Wednesday and Saturday evenings. The zoo's After-Hours Tour is a chance to peek behind the curtain, feed the otters, touch a reptile, and more. The two-hour tour, which begins at 8 P.M. April–September and 6 P.M. October–March, costs $35 per person. Participants must pre-register 72 hours in advance. ZooAmerica is connected to Hersheypark by a walking bridge. It also has a year-round, dedicated entrance on Park Avenue (Route 743).

Hershey's Chocolate World

When The Hershey Company ceased stopped factory tours in the 1970s, it gave the public Hershey's Chocolate World (251 Park Blvd., Hershey, 717/534-4900, www.hersheys.com/ chocolateworld, open year-round, hours vary). Adjacent to Hersheypark, Chocolate World is part mall, part interactive museum. Its shops sell anything and everything Hershey's, including pillows shaped like packets of Reese's Peanut Butter Cups, Twizzlers-shaped pens, and personalized chocolate bars. A primer on the chocolate-making process is available in

MILTON HERSHEY'S ORPHAN HEIRS

Married for 10 years and unable to have children, Milton Hershey and his wife, Catherine, established a boarding school for orphaned boys in 1909. The Hershey Industrial School, as it was called at the time, had an initial enrollment of 10. Catherine Hershey – "Kitty" to her adoring husband – wouldn't live to see its dramatic expansion. After a long and debilitating muscular illness, she died in 1915. Three years later, Milton Hershey transferred the bulk of his fortune, including his stock in the Hershey Chocolate Company, to the trust created to fund the school. Upon his death in 1945, townspeople streamed into the school's foyer, where his body lay in state. The funeral service was held in the auditorium, with eight boys from the senior class serving as pallbearers.

Renamed the Milton Hershey School (www.mhs-pa.org) in 1951, it began enrolling girls in the 1970s. Today more than 1,200 underprivileged children from pre-kindergarten through 12th grade live and learn on the 9,000-acre campus – at no cost to their families. Milton Hershey's endowment has grown in value to more than $6 billion. The school trust's assets include a 30 percent stake in the Hershey Company and full ownership of Hershey Entertainment & Resorts, the company that runs Hersheypark, ZooAmerica, The Hotel Hershey, the Giant Center, the Hershey Theatre, and other products of Milton Hershey's vision of a town rich in recreational and cultural resources.

the form of a slow-moving amusement ride. Passengers are transported from a tropical rainforest where cocoa beans flourish to a chocolate factory, encountering some singing cows along the way. The ride is free, as is a sample of a Hershey's confection at its conclusion. Other Chocolate World attractions have an admission fee. The Hershey's Really Big 3-D Show, an animated musical complete with rumbling seats and smoke plumes, is $5.95 for adults, $5.45 for seniors, $4.95 for children 3–12. The Chocolate Tasting Adventure, a chance to compare various chocolates under the tutelage of an expert, is $9.95 for adults, $9.45 for seniors, $6.95 for children. Call for tasting times.

To fill up on something other than candy, head to the food court or the Kit Kat "Gimme a Break" Café, which serves hot dogs, sandwiches, nachos, and the like. If you buy nothing else during your visit to Chocolate World, buy a chocolate milkshake. Worth every calorie.

Complimentary shuttle service is available from Chocolate World to The Hershey Story and ZooAmerica. You can also hop aboard an old-fashioned trolley car for a fascinating tour of the town with a ham of a conductor. **Hershey Trolley Works** (717/533-3000, www.hersheytrolleyworks.com, fare $12.95, seniors $11.95, children 3–12 $5.95) tours depart Chocolate World daily rain or shine.

Hershey Gardens

When chocolate magnate and philanthropist Milton Hershey was asked to sponsor a national rosarium in Washington D.C., he decided to create one in his eponymous town instead. "A nice garden of roses," as he called it, opened to the public in 1937 and within five years had blossomed into a 23-acre horticultural haven. Roses are still the specialty at Hershey Gardens (170 Hotel Rd., Hershey, 717/534-3492, www.hersheygardens.org, open daily late Mar.–Oct. and Fri.–Sun. Nov.–Dec., hours vary, admission $10, seniors $9, children 3–12 $6), located across from The Hotel Hershey. More than 7,000 roses of 275 varieties bloom during the summer months. Springtime is pretty special too. That's when 30,000 tulips of 100 varieties blanket the Seasonal Display Garden and daffodils light up the Perennial Garden. Bold-colored chrysanthemums steal the show in fall. But what most visitors go ga-ga over isn't roses or tulips or any flower for that matter. It's the Butterfly House, open from late May through late September. Visitors can observe the entire lifecycle of the ethereal insects. Also popular is the Children's Garden, filled with not only flora but also fun activities.

The Hotel Hershey

The Hotel Hershey (100 Hotel Rd., Hershey, 717/533-2171, www.thehotelhershey.com), a Mediterranean-style product of Milton Hershey's Depression-era building campaign, deserves a spot on your itinerary even if you're not staying there. Grand to begin with, the hotel is grander than ever on the heels of a $67 million renovation and expansion. Some amenities, like the year-round ice-skating rink unveiled in 2009, are exclusively for guests. But nonguests can still have a field day. For starters, they can sink into a chocolate milk bath at The Spa at The Hotel Hershey (717/520-5888,

The Hotel Hershey

a king room at The Hotel Hershey

www.chocolatespa.com), better known by its nickname, the **Chocolate Spa.** Other chocolate-inspired services include a Swedish massage with chocolate-scented oil and an exfoliating treatment with cocoa bean husks. The spa menu also pays homage to Cuba, where Milton Hershey spent much of his time after his wife's death in 1915, buying and building sugar mills. The Noche Azul Soak, for example, is a 15-minute dip in waters infused with Cuba's national flower. The three-story spa overlooks the hotel's formal gardens and reflecting pools.

The hotel's boutiques welcome the general public. Among them is a swimwear store with a particularly large selection of chocolate-brown pieces and a sweets shop where customers can decorate their own cupcakes. One of the oldest and most distinguished restaurants in central Pennsylvania calls the hotel home. The **Circular Dining Room** (breakfast 7–10:30 A.M. daily, brunch noon–2:30 P.M. Sun., dinner 5:30–9 P.M. Mon.–Sat. and 6–9 P.M. Sun., call for lunch hours, dinner $28–39) owes its shape to Milton Hershey, who noticed during his world travels

that guests who tipped poorly were often seated in the corners of restaurants. "I don't want any corners," he reportedly said. He also saw to it that the restaurant had no pillars, having noticed that single diners were often seated at tables with obstructed views. A recent addition to the hotel's dining portfolio, **Harvest** (717/534-8800, 11:30 A.M.–10 P.M. daily, $9–28) offers regional American cuisine made with ingredients found within a 100-mile radius of the hotel. Not interested in spa treatments, shopping, or excellent food? Come to The Hotel Hershey for the view. Situated on a hilltop, it overlooks "The Sweetest Place on Earth."

Antique Auto Museum at Hershey

Home to the Lakeland bus used in the movie *Forrest Gump* and a green Cadillac Seville once owned by actress Betty White, the Antique Auto Museum at Hershey (161 Museum Dr., Hershey, 717/566-7100, www.aacamuseum .org, 9 A.M.–5 P.M. daily, admission $10, seniors $9, children 4–12 $7) is one of the few

© HERSHEYHARRISBURG.COM

Antique Auto Museum at Hershey

attractions in town that have nothing to do with chocolate. An affiliate of the Smithsonian Institution, the museum displays more than 150 cars, motorcycles, and buses—many in elaborate dioramas depicting scenes such as a turn-of-the-20th-century machine shop, a 1940s gas station, and a 1950s drive-in. A highlight of the cruise through time is a restored 1941 Valentine Diner relocated from Wichita, Kansas. The museum frequently stages special exhibitions of loaned vehicles. Among its recent borrowings: turbine-powered, aeronautically inspired concept cars from the General Motors Heritage Center, a pair of stainless steel cars created in the 1960s, and a 1953 Cadillac LeMans, one of only four built and two known to exist. On the first Saturday of each month and throughout the holiday season, visitors can check out the museum's model train display, a miniaturization of small-town America in the 1950s.

Indian Echo Caverns

Geological forces make for family entertainment at Indian Echo Caverns (368 Middletown Rd., Hummelstown, 717/566-8131, www.indian echocaverns.com, 9 A.M.–6 P.M. daily Memorial Day–Labor Day, 10 A.M.–4 P.M. rest of year, admission $13, seniors $11, children 3–11 $7), located four miles west of Hershey off U.S. 322. The first visitors to the limestone caverns were likely Susquehannock Indians seeking shelter from inclement weather. The caverns still do a brisk business on rainy days, when Hersheypark holds less than its usual appeal. Guides point out spectacular formations and share cavern lore during 45-minute walking tours. It's always a cool 52 degrees inside, so dress accordingly. In summer, allot an extra hour if you're bringing kids. The grounds include a playground, a petting zoo, and Gem Mill Junction, where budding prospectors can search for amethyst, jasper, agate, and other treasures.

Hollywood Casino at Penn National Race Course

Not every attraction in the Hershey area was built with kids in mind. Nine miles north of chocolate central, grownups gamble on slots and horses at Hollywood Casino at Penn National Race Course (77 Hollywood Blvd., Grantville, 717/469-2211, www.hcpn.com, open 24 hours). Live thoroughbred races, a tradition since 1972, are held Wednesday–Saturday evenings throughout the year as well as most Tuesdays May–July. The casino, which opened in 2008, is ding-ding-ding 24/7 with the occasional ka-ching! Its 2,300-plus slot machines range from penny slots to $100 slots. Dining options include the upscale **Final Cut Steakhouse** (717/469-3090, 5:30–10 P.M. Wed.–Sat., 4–9 P.M. Sun., $25–42), with a menu biased toward Hereford beef but not averse to lobster tails, grass-fed lamb, and Cornish game hen. There's a buffet restaurant, of course. Lunch is $12.99, dinner $19.99.

Cornwall Iron Furnace

Cornwall Iron Furnace (94 Rexmont Rd., Cornwall, 717/272-9711, www.cornwall ironfurnace.org, 9 A.M.–5 P.M. Thurs.–Sat., noon–5 P.M. Sun., admission $6, seniors $5.50, children 3–11 $4) was retired from service more than a century ago, but it still has a job to do: teaching visitors about the fiery infancy of America's metals industry. Charcoal-fueled furnaces dotted the Pennsylvania countryside in the 18th and 19th centuries, but this one is unique in its intactness. Indeed, the blast furnace and related buildings are regarded as one of the best-preserved 19th-century ironmaking complexes in the world.

Stonemason Peter Grubb established the furnace in 1742, naming the area Cornwall after a region of England. For more than a century and a half, the furnace consumed copious amounts of charcoal, iron ore, and limestone, producing molten iron that was cast into cannons, stoves, and other products. It was abandoned in 1883, rendered obsolete by coal-fueled ironmaking operations. Today the furnace looks much as it did following extensive renovations in the mid-1800s. What used to be the charcoal barn is now a visitors center with interpretive exhibits on mining, charcoal-making, and ironmaking. Other surviving structures include a blacksmith shop, a building where wagons were built

and repaired, and a darling Gothic Revival building that served as a butcher shop for the ironmaster's estate. The iron ore mine, which continued to operate until 1973, is just south of the furnace site and visible from Boyd Street. The open pit mine was sensationally prolific, yielding more than 100 million tons before beginning to flood. Today it's filled with water. Houses built in the 19th century for miners and furnace workers still line Boyd Street.

ENTERTAINMENT AND EVENTS
Performance Venues

Best known as the home arena of the Hershey Bears hockey team, **Giant Center** (550 W. Hersheypark Dr., Hershey, 717/534-3911, www.giantcenter.com) hosts some of the flashiest performers to pass through Hershey. It opened in 2002 with a Cher concert. More recent guests have included 50 Cent, Kelly Clarkson, the Harlem Globetrotters, the Ringling Bros. and Barnum & Bailey circus, and Republican running mates John McCain and Sarah Palin, who held a rally there during the 2008 presidential race. Less-than-famous folks can hit the ice during occasional public skating sessions. The arena seats 10,000–12,500 depending on the nature of the event.

Hersheypark Stadium (100 W. Hersheypark Dr., Hershey, 717/534-3911) can accommodate 30,000 fans for concerts. The outdoor stadium has hosted the likes of The Who, James Taylor, Alabama, U2, Dave Matthews Band, and an 'N Sync 'n' Pink doubleheader. It's also the venue for sporting events such as the Big 33 Football Classic, an annual all-star game between high school players from Pennsylvania and Ohio. Built as part of Milton Hershey's Depression-era building campaign, the stadium at one point served as the summer home of the Philadelphia Eagles. **The Star Pavilion** opened at Hersheypark Stadium in 1996. It's a more intimate open-air venue with reserved and lawn seating for 8,000.

The spectacular **Hershey Theatre** (15 E. Caracas Ave., Hershey, 717/534-3405, www .hersheytheatre.com) also went up during

Mr. Hershey's "Great Building Campaign," which created jobs for an estimated 600 skilled workers. And skilled they were. The lobby boasts a floor laid with polished Italian lava rock, soaring marble arches, and a ceiling adorned with bas-relief images of swans, war chariots, and more. The foyer and auditorium reveal the architect's fondness for Venice, Italy. A winged lion, the symbol of Venice, is mounted above the stage, and the proscenium arch calls to mind an ancient canal bridge. An intricate lighting system creates the illusion of twinkling stars and floating clouds overhead. The 1,904-seat theater hosts touring Broadway shows, concerts, dance performances, and classic films.

If you catch a concert at Giant Center, Hersheypark Stadium, The Star Pavilion, or the Hershey Theatre during Hersheypark's May–September season, you can present your ticket or ticket stub at the amusement park's front gate for a discounted admission price of $33.95. The discount applies the day before, day of, and day after the concert.

Festivals and Events

With Hersheypark closed and temps that dip below freezing, February wouldn't seem like a good time to visit Hershey. If you're a bargain-hunting chocolate lover, it's an ideal time. Each day of **Chocolate-Covered February** (800/437-7439, www.chocolatecovered february.com) brings a host of chocolate-themed activities along with discounts on everything from museum tickets to spa treatments. The month-long celebration of Hershey's signature foodstuff features chocolate-inspired meals, chef demonstrations, and classes in topics such as truffle-making, chocolate martini mixology, and wine and chocolate pairing.

There's no shortage of entertainment in Hershey during the summer months, but fans of classical and jazz music may wish to head east, to Mount Gretna. The resort community about 12 miles from Hershey has long been known as a cultural mecca. It's home to the **Pennsylvania Chautauqua** (general information 717/964-3270, summer programs 717/964-1830, www.pachautauqua.org), which sponsors Thursday evening organ recitals, Sunday evening "mini concerts," and a host of other cultural and educational programs throughout the summer. **Music at Gretna** (717/361-1508, www.gretnamusic.org), a classical chamber music and jazz festival spanning several weeks, has welcomed the likes of jazz pianist Dave Brubeck and singer/guitarist John Pizzarelli.

Hershey welcomes thousands of antique automobile enthusiasts during the first full week of October. The **Antique Automobile Club of America's Eastern Division National Fall Meet** (717/566-7720, www.hersheyaaca.org), held in Hershey since 1955, is one of the largest antique automobile shows and flea markets in the country.

SHOPPING

The **Outlets at Hershey** (46 Outlet Square, Hershey, 717/520-1236, www.theoutletsat hershey.com, 9:30 A.M.–6 P.M. Mon.–Thurs., 9:30 A.M.–9 P.M. Fri.–Sat., 11 A.M.–5 P.M. Sun.) are just off Hershey Park Drive, within minutes of Hersheypark and other main attractions. The outlet center's 60-some stores include Brooks Brothers, J. Crew, Liz Claiborne, Calvin Klein, Tommy Hilfiger, and Polo Ralph Lauren.

SPORTS AND RECREATION
Spectator Sports

The **Hershey Bears** (Giant Center, 550 W. Hersheypark Dr., Hershey, 717/534-3380, www.hersheybears.com) have competed in the professional American Hockey League without interruption since 1938. Amateur hockey came to Hershey even earlier, in 1931. The popularity of matches between college teams convinced chocolate czar Milton S. Hershey and his longtime chief of entertainment and amusements, John B. Sollenberger, to sponsor a permanent team the following year. They called it the Hershey B'ars and dressed the players in maroon and silver—just like the Hershey Bar. Renamed the Hershey Bears in 1936, the team has brought home at least one Calder

Cup, the AHL's ultimate prize, every decade since the 1940s. The Bears "draw more fans and inspire more passion than just about any team in minor league hockey," *The Washington Post* wrote of the Washington Capitals' affiliate in 2009. Later that year, the Bears became the first team in league history to win 10 championships.

Top high school athletes and their families frequently descend on Hershey. The town hosts the **Big 33 Football Classic** (717/774-3303, www.big33.org), an all-star game that pits Pennsylvania's best against Ohio's, as well as various Pennsylvania Interscholastic Athletic Association (717/697-0374, www.piaa.org) championships.

ACCOMMODATIONS

Hershey Entertainment & Resorts (800/437-7439, www.hersheypa.com), the company founded when Milton Hershey decided to separate his non-chocolate ventures from the business that made them all possible, controls not only most of the tourist attractions in town but also three lodging properties: the upscale Hotel Hershey, the more affordable Hershey Lodge, and the Hershey Highmeadow Campground. There are plenty of other places to bed down, but staying at a Hershey Resorts property has its privileges. Guests of the Hotel Hershey and Hershey Lodge get free admission to the Hershey Gardens and The Hershey Story, while campground guests get discounted admission. Other perks include free seasonal shuttle service to Hersheypark and access to some rides before the gates officially open. Hershey Resorts guests also have the exclusive opportunity to purchase a Hersheypark Sweet Access Pass, bearers of which can cut to the front of most lines and otherwise behave like VIPs.

For obvious reasons, most Hershey hotels charge a heckuva lot more in summer than the rest of the year.

Under $100
Open year-round, **Hershey Highmeadow Campground** (1200 Matlack Rd.,

Hummelstown, 717/534-8999, www.hershey camping.com, campsites $30–51, cabins $68–135) offers more than 300 tent and RV sites and cabins ranging from rustic to deluxe. The 55-acre campground is minutes from Hersheypark. Amenities include two swimming pools, a game room, basketball and volleyball courts, horseshoe pits, and a country store. Organized activities add to the fun in summer. The campground has 22 cabins without indoor plumbing, plus two deluxe cabins complete with kitchen and bathroom. Cabins sleep anywhere from four to eight people. Campsite and cabin rates are based on occupancy of up to four. There's a $5 per night fee for each additional person. Another good budget option: the family-run **Chocolatetown Motel** (1806 E. Chocolate Ave., Hershey, 717/533-2330, www.chocolatetownmotel.com, $54–140). Even during the busiest weeks of the busy season, rates start at just $89. An outdoor pool adds to its appeal.

$100-300
With 665 guest rooms and suites and 100,000 square feet of function space, **◖ Hershey Lodge** (325 University Dr., Hershey, 717/533-3311, www.hersheylodge.com, summer $290–310, off-season $170–270) is Pennsylvania's largest convention resort. Not surprisingly, it's quite often crawling with convention-goers. But it's also wildly popular with families, won over by amenities including an 18-hole miniature golf course, activities such as poolside movies and family bingo, and appearances by Hershey's product characters. (Who can resist a huggable Hershey's Kiss?) The chocolate theme extends to the decor of the guest rooms, which feature complimentary wireless internet access, refrigerators, and flat-screen TVs. Guests can catch A&E Biography's *Milton Hershey: The Chocolate King* any time of day.

Hershey has several chain hotels in this price range. Closest to the action: **Days Inn Hershey** (350 W. Chocolate Ave., Hershey, 717/534-2162, www.daysinnhershey.com, summer $200–270, off-season $110–160). Owned and operated by a lifelong Hershey resident, the hotel has more to recommend it than convenience. The rooms are spacious and the staff gracious. On-site massages are available. Guests get all sorts of freebies: hotel-wide wireless Internet access, continental breakfast, shuttle service to Hersheypark, 24-hour coffee service, and use of the Gold's Gym less than two miles away. Plus, they get to bring their pets.

Another fine choice is **SpringHill Suites Hershey** (115 Museum Dr., Hershey, 717/583-2222, www.springhillsuiteshershey.com, summer $250–260, off-season $125–160), where Internet access and breakfast are likewise free. It's next door to the Antique Auto Museum and fairly new, having opened in 2000. All guest rooms are studio-suites with a pull-out sofa in addition to one or two beds. Both the Days Inn and SpringHill Suites have an indoor pool and whirlpool, a fitness center, and guest laundry facilities.

For homier digs, head to the **1825 Inn Bed & Breakfast** (409 S. Lingle Ave., Palmyra, 717/838-8282, www.1825inn.com, $114–239). The main house has six country-style guest rooms with private baths. A pair of cottages with a more contemporary aesthetic, king-sized beds, two-person Jacuzzis, and private decks seem to have been designed with honeymooners in mind.

Some of the area's most elegant accommodations can be found on a picturesque horse farm. **⊏ The Inn at Westwynd Farm** (1620 Sand Beach Rd., Hummelstown, 717/533-6764, www.westwyndfarminn.com, $109–259) is just 10 minutes north of Hershey but, as owners Carolyn and Frank Troxell are fond of saying, "a world apart." Their goal is simple: to pamper the heck out of guests. That means refreshments upon arrival, a bottomless cookie jar, and gourmet breakfasts that reflect the season, often flavored with herbs from their own garden. The Troxells are happy to point guests to good restaurants and even arrange for a dinner at the home of an Amish family. Bringing your family? Ask for the carriage house with its full bath, living room, and space enough for six. The main house has nine en suite guest

rooms, eight of which have fireplaces, five of which have Jacuzzis, and all of which have charm in spades.

Over $300

Milton Hershey's plan to build a luxury hotel in the midst of the Great Depression met with ridicule. He poured $2 million into the project anyway. When he addressed the first guests of **The Hotel Hershey** (100 Hotel Rd., Hershey, 717/533-2171, www.thehotelhershey.com, summer traditional room $370–430, cottage room $500–535, off-season traditional room $250–390, cottage room $400–495) on May 26, 1933, he also addressed his critics. "When we farmers go to the city, we are impressed by the fine hotels we see there," he said. "So I thought I'd impress the city folks by building a fine hotel on one of our farms. I am of the opinion that there will be a need for this hotel someday, although the prospects do not look very encouraging at the present time." Mr. Hershey's 170-room hotel impressed folks, indeed. Renowned newsman Lowell Thomas, who visited the hotel in its first year, described it as "a palace that out-palaces the palaces of the Maharajahs of India." The Hotel Hershey is even more palatial now, having treated itself to a $67 million facelift and expansion on the occasion of its 75th anniversary. Among the new facilities is an outdoor swimming complex with an infinity-edge pool for grown-ups, a family pool with two large slides, a whirlpool, and an eatery. The pool complex also has 14 swanky cabanas complete with flat-screen TVs, ceiling fans, and refrigerators, available to guests for $200 a day. (The hotel has an indoor pool, so guests can still get their swim on during the colder months.) Also added as part of the expansion: an all-weather ice-skating rink, seven boutique shops, and 10 luxury guest cottages. Bordering dense woods, the four- and six-bedroom cottages are the hotel's poshest accommodations. Guests can reserve individual bedrooms or an entire cottage. The latter affords them access to a great room with a fireplace, French doors opening to a porch, and

pool complex at The Hotel Hershey

other comforts. The hotel's main building has 230 guest rooms and suites, including the especially elegant Milton Hershey Suite with its veranda overlooking the town of Hershey.

FOOD

Two of Hershey's best restaurants are within The Hotel Hershey (100 Hotel Rd., Hershey, restaurant reservations 717/534-8800, www .thehotelhershey.com). Fancier of the two is the **C Circular Dining Room** (breakfast 7–10:30 A.M. daily, brunch noon–2:30 P.M. Sun., dinner 5:30–9 P.M. Mon.–Sat. and 6–9 P.M. Sun., call for lunch hours, dinner $28–39), which dates to the 1930s. Built without corners or pillars as per Milton Hershey's instructions, the restaurant recently underwent a $1 million renovation that included the addition of a 1,200-bottle wine cellar. Its wine list now offers some 350 labels. The dinner menu changes with the seasons and, not surprisingly, makes liberal use of chocolate and cocoa. What may surprise first-time

guests is their use in dishes savory as well as sweet—dishes such as cocoa-seared jumbo scallops and venison chop with cocoa nib jus. On Friday evenings the restaurant offers a six-course chef's tasting menu for $75. The Circular Dining Room's greatest claim to fame is its Sunday brunch. At $39.95 per person (kids 3–8 can dive in for $19.50), the gourmet smorgasbord isn't cheap. But it's possible to eat your money's worth with a couple of trips to the fresh seafood bar. Reservations are required for the Sunday brunch, lunch buffet ($23 per person, children 3–8 $11.50), and dinner. Gentlemen need a jacket and ladies a dress or dress pants for Sunday brunch and dinner. "Resort casual" rules the day at **Harvest** (11:30 A.M.–10 P.M. daily, $9–28), which joined The Hotel Hershey's menu of eateries in 2009. The folks at Harvest are fiercely loyal to local growers and producers, so much so that even the pretzels crushed to coat its chicken tenders hail from within a 100-mile radius of the hotel. Both lunch and dinner menus offer a variety of salads, sandwiches, burgers, and entrées.

Fenicci's of Hershey (102 W. Chocolate Ave., Hershey, 717/533-7159, www.feniccis.com, 11 A.M.–midnight Mon.–Thurs., 11 A.M.–1 A.M. Fri.–Sat., noon–11 P.M. Sun., $9–28) is spitting distance from Hersheypark, The Hershey Story, and other main attractions, but don't mistake it for a tourist trap. The casual Italian eatery, which dates to 1935, is beloved by generations of locals. It's famous for its upside-down pizza—cheese on bottom, sauce on top—and its homemade meat, marinara, and mushroom sauces. The Italian wedding soup, made daily, is also a hit. The menu is extensive, with five risottos, six parms, and scores of variations on pasta. There's a kids' menu too. Grown-ups have the benefit of a full bar and live music on Friday and Saturday nights.

Also popular with locals, **Fire Alley** (1144 Cocoa Ave., Hershey, 717/533-3200, www.firealley.net, 4–10 P.M. Sun.–Thurs., 4–11 P.M. Fri.–Sat., bar closes later, $7–28) is an offshoot of Harrisburg's Fire House, which occupies a restored 19th-century firehouse. What Fire Alley lacks in historical value it makes up for in style. Inside the suburban eatery, murals, awnings, window boxes, and streetlights create the impression of an urban streetscape, complete with graffiti. Fire Alley's cleverest design element is banquette-styling seating at the bar: all the comfort of a booth with readier access to the bartender. It's the food, of course, that accounts for the large roster of regulars. The kitchen does wings, burgers, veal parmesan—stuff you'd expect from a casual eatery—but also mussels steamed in Guinness, seared tuna on seaweed salad, and slow-roasted prime rib. The meatloaf is swaddled in bacon, and the nachos fall in the seafood category. Drop by on a Thursday for $4 margaritas.

The curiously named **What If . . .** (845 E. Chocolate Ave., Hershey, 717/533-5858, www.whatifdining.com, 11 A.M.–10 P.M. Mon.–Thurs., 11 A.M.–11 P.M. Fri.–Sat., 4–10 P.M. Sun., bar menu available for an additional hour Memorial Day–Labor Day $7–32) is in an off-putting location: below street level in the Howard Johnson Inn Hershey. But if you can overlook the lack of natural light, you'll be glad you came. Start with the crab martini and end with the profiterole du jour, made in-house along with every other dessert. In between, tuck into an entrée from the menu of continental cuisine. The extensive wine list is partial to California and the Pacific Northwest.

INFORMATION

The **Hershey Harrisburg Regional Visitors Bureau** (17 S. 2nd St., Harrisburg, 717/231-7788, www.hersheyharrisburg.org, 9 A.M.–5 P.M. Mon.–Fri. and 10 A.M.–3 P.M. Sat., also open 10 A.M.–2 P.M. Sun. in summer) has loads of information about attractions, lodging, and dining in and around Hershey. Visit the bureau's website to request a copy of its current visitors guide or peruse a digital version. For information about Pennsylvania Dutch Country as a whole, visit www.dutchcountryroads.com.

GETTING THERE AND AROUND

Hershey is about 30 miles northwest of Lancaster and 15 miles east of Harrisburg, the state capital. **Harrisburg International Airport** (888/235-9442, www.flyhia.com), about a 20-minute drive from Hershey, is served by Air Canada, AirTran Airways, Continental Airlines, Delta Air Lines, United Airlines, and US Airways. They offer daily nonstop service to about a dozen destinations. Note that while locals refer to the airport as HIA, its Federal Aviation Administration booking code is MDT. That's because of its physical location in the borough of Middletown, about eight miles south of Harrisburg.

Harrisburg is served by **Amtrak** (800/872-7245, www.amtrak.com) and intercity bus companies. Once there, rent a car or hop in a cab to get to Hershey. You can also travel to Hershey from Harrisburg by **Capital Area Transit** (717/238-8304, www.cattransit.com) bus.

Harrisburg and Vicinity

Like many state capitals, Harrisburg isn't much of a vacation destination. It's awfully close to one; Hershey, a.k.a. Chocolate Town, USA, is just 15 miles to its east. Most people come to Harrisburg because they have business there, and more often than not, it's government business. That's not to say there's nothing to see or do in the city, which lies on the east bank of the Susquehanna River. Harrisburg has some excellent museums, including the State Museum of Pennsylvania and the National Civil War Museum. It has a charming park along the river and another *on* the river. It has more minor league teams than you can imagine. In recent years the dining and nightlife scenes have improved to such a degree that it's not unusual for innkeepers in the Hershey area to point guests toward Harrisburg for dinner.

The city owes its name to John Harris, who emigrated from England in the late 17th century, built a home on the river near the present juncture of Paxton and Front Streets, and eventually established the first ferry across the Susquehanna. The ferry played an important role in the westward migration of other pioneers and later in the Revolutionary War, carrying supplies to the Continental army west of the Susquehanna. After the war, John Harris Jr. made plans for a town on his father's land, which had come to be known as Harris's Ferry. Freshly named, Harrisburg was incorporated in 1791. In 1812, it replaced Lancaster as the state capital.

Over the next several decades, Harrisburg emerged as a transportation center, first as a linchpin of Pennsylvania's canal system and then as a railroad hub. During the Civil War, the rail yards teemed with Union soldiers. Hundreds of thousands of men received their instructions at Harrisburg's Camp Curtin. With its transportation arteries and trove of supplies, Harrisburg was a target for Confederate General Robert E. Lee. His troops might have captured the vulnerable capital

Harrisburg skyline

in 1863—they made it as far as Camp Hill, just across the river—had they not received an urgent order to turn south. The Battle of Gettysburg was at hand.

More than a century later, the citizens of Harrisburg would feel threatened once again. In March 1979, the Three Mile Island nuclear power plant, about 15 miles south of the capital, suffered a partial meltdown. Tens of thousands of people fled their homes. The sight of the plant's cooling towers is still somewhat chilling. Current owner Exelon Corp. occasionally invites the public to visit and see that everything is hunky-dory.

It's best to visit Harrisburg during the warmer months, when the Susquehanna calls to boaters and anglers and the riverfront hosts one festival after another. Be sure to venture outside the city. Take a trip on the only remaining ferry across the Susquehanna. Take a hike on the Appalachian Trail. If nothing else, take a look at the city from across the river. Not bad for a place that's rarely seen on postcards.

SIGHTS
Whitaker Center for Science and the Arts
Part science museum, part performing arts center, and part movie theater, the Whitaker Center (222 Market St., Harrisburg, 717/214-2787, www.whitakercenter.org, 9:30 A.M.–5 P.M. Tues.–Sat., 11:30 A.M.–5 P.M. Sun., admission Science Center only $13.75, seniors, students, and children 3–12 $11.75) is downtown Harrisburg's cultural hub. The $53 million center, which opened in 1999, houses the Sunoco Performance Theater and an IMAX theater with an 80-foot-wide screen—the largest in central Pennsylvania. It's also home to the Harsco Science Center, three floors of exhibits about everything from weather systems to the physics of dance. Visitors can venture a hand into a writhing eight-foot-tall tornado, test their physical and mental fitness, assemble telescopes and microscopes, discover how dancers manipulate their center of gravity to appear to be floating during leaps, and more. KidsPlace, a gallery for children 5 and under,

opened in 2008 and features a miniature version of Harrisburg's Broad Street Market, the oldest continuously operated market house in the United States. Other exhibits with a local twist include a model of the Susquehanna River, which passes within a few blocks of the Whitaker Center. Combo tickets for Science Center visitors who want to catch an IMAX documentary are $17.75 for adults and $15.75 for seniors, students with ID, and children 3–12. Hollywood movies shown on the giant screen are $13.75 for adults and $11.75 for seniors, students, and children.

State Museum of Pennsylvania
Free for more than a century, the State Museum of Pennsylvania (300 North St., Harrisburg, 717/787-4980, www.statemuseumpa.org, 9 A.M.–5 P.M. Thurs.–Sat., noon–5 P.M. Sun., admission $5, seniors and children 1–12 $4) implemented an admission fee in mid-2009, citing "budget considerations." But it's still a bargain (and still free on the third Saturday of every month). The four-story circular museum next to the State Capitol offers a well-rounded perspective on Pennsylvania's story. The Hall of Paleontology and Geology introduces visitors to earlier life forms, including a massive armored fish that prowled the seas of Pennsylvania and Ohio some 367 million years ago and the Marshalls Creek Mastodon, a prehistoric elephant whose remains were discovered in the small eastern Pennsylvania community after which it's named. Also popular is the Hall of Mammals, a set of 13 life-sized dioramas of native animals in their natural environments. The Civil War gallery features Peter Rothermel's famous painting of Pickett's Charge at the Battle of Gettysburg. Unveiled in 1870, the plus-sized masterpiece (32 feet long and almost 17 feet high) toured the country, appearing at the World's Fair in Philadelphia in 1876. Though it garnered much praise, it also came under fire. Critics complained that the dying Union soldiers had angelic countenances while the rebels appeared wracked with guilt.

Access to Curiosity Connection, a play area designed for children ages 1–5, is included in

© HERSHEYHARRISBURG.ORG

the State Museum of Pennsylvania in Harrisburg

general admission. The State Museum also houses a planetarium. Planetarium tickets, which include museum admission, are $7 for adults and $6 for seniors and children 12 and under. Additional planetarium shows are $2.

Susquehanna Art Museum

Dismayed that the state capital had no art museum, four art educators set about making one in 1989. Today the Susquehanna Art Museum (301 Market St., Harrisburg, 717/233-8668, www.sqart.org, 10 A.M.–4 P.M. Tues.–Wed. and Fri.–Sat., 4–8 P.M. Thurs., 1–4 P.M. Sun., admission $5, seniors and students $3, children 12 and under free) occupies the first three floors of the Kunkel Building, kitty-corner from the Whitaker Center. Each year, the museum stages four exhibits of museum-quality pieces by internationally recognized artists. Its Doshi Gallery for Contemporary Art, located on the second floor, showcases the works of regional artists.

Civil War Sights

Though enemy forces failed to reach it, Harrisburg was not untouched by the Civil War.

Far from it. The city was a major transportation hub for the North's war effort. Only Baltimore and Washington had more soldiers pass through their railroad stations. It was also a strategic center. More than 300,000 men were processed through **Camp Curtin,** which opened in April 1861 on what was then the northern outskirts of Harrisburg. The Union's first and largest training facility, named for Pennsylvania's governor at the time, closed in November 1865, seven months after the Confederacy surrendered. Today a statue of Governor Andrew G. Curtin stands in a small park one block north of the intersection of Maclay and North Sixth Streets, where soldiers entered the camp. Local citizens donated food and other supplies for the soldiers streaming through Harrisburg. The Ladies Union Relief Association raised funds, knitted socks, and tended the wounded. Fallen Union soldiers were buried at the **Harrisburg Cemetery** at Liberty and North 13th Streets on the eastern end of the city. Established in 1845, the 350-acre cemetery is also the final resting place of some Revolutionary War soldiers and Pennsylvania governors.

At the end of the war, tens of thousands of Union soldiers paraded through the streets of Washington, D.C., past joyous crowds toward a reviewing stand in front of the White House. Excluded from the Grand Review of the Armies were the regiments of the U.S. Colored Troops, including 11 from Pennsylvania. In November 1865, a parade honoring them was held in Harrisburg. African American veterans marched from State and Filbert Streets on the east side of the Capitol to the Front Street home of Simon Cameron, a longtime abolitionist who'd served in the U.S. Senate and, for a spell, as President Abraham Lincoln's secretary of war. He reviewed them from his front porch and delivered a speech in which he promised: "If you continue to conduct yourselves hereafter as you have in this struggle, you will have all the rights you ask for, all the rights that belong to human beings." No other state held such an event. Cameron's residence was donated to the Historical Society of Dauphin County in 1941 and is now known as the **John Harris-Simon Cameron Mansion** (219 S. Front St., Harrisburg, 717/233-3462, www

.dauphincountyhistory.org, 1–4 P.M. Tues.–Fri. and second Sat. of the month Apr.–mid-Dec., admission $8, seniors $7, children 6–16 $6). The house has undergone many additions and renovations since it was built in the mid-1700s for John Harris Jr., who founded Harrisburg on land his father had settled. Cameron was responsible for its makeover into an Italianate-style Victorian, adding a grand staircase and solarium and lowering the floor in the front section of the house by 3 feet to accommodate a pair of 14-foot-tall pier mirrors he'd found in France. Guided tours reveal what else he snapped up on his way to Russia, where he was sent as U.S. ambassador after his scandal-marred stint as war secretary.

Harrisburg's premier Civil War attraction opened in 2001. The **National Civil War Museum** (1 Lincoln Circle at Reservoir Park, Harrisburg, 717/260-1861, www.national civilwarmuseum.org, 10 A.M.–5 P.M. Mon.–Tues. and Thurs.–Sat., 10 A.M.–8 P.M. Wed., noon–5 P.M. Sun., admission $9, seniors $8, students $7, family pass $35) bills itself as a bias-free presentation of the Union and

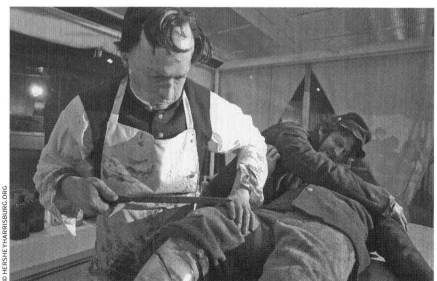

Realistic mannequins graphically depict Civil War-era life at the National Civil War Museum.

Confederate causes, "the only museum in the United States that portrays the entire story of the American Civil War." Its focus isn't on the famous—President Lincoln, General Robert E. Lee, and such—but on the common soldier and the men and women on the home front. Particular attention is paid to the African American experience. Lifelike mannequins star in depictions of a slave auction, soldier life at Camp Curtin, the amputation of a soldier's leg, and other facts of 19th-century life.

If you just can't get enough of Civil War history, visit www.dutchcountryroads.com and download the *Pennsylvania Civil War Trails* brochure or request that one be sent to you. The brochure will direct you to places of significance along two routes, one starting in Harrisburg and the other in Gettysburg.

Pennsylvania State Capitol

Completed in 1906, the current Capitol (N. 3rd St., between North and Walnut Streets, 800/868-7672, www.pacapitol.com) was the tallest structure between Philadelphia and Pittsburgh for 80 years. It's still among the most ornate. The seat of state power features a spectacular vaulted dome inspired by Michelangelo's design for St. Peter's Basilica in Rome. Architect Joseph Huston incorporated elements of Greek, Roman, Renaissance, and Victorian design into the building, envisioning a "palace of arts." His vision cost a pretty penny, and Huston was sentenced to prison for overcharging the state. There's no charge for guided tours of the Capitol, part of a large complex of government buildings. They're offered every half hour 8:30 A.M.–4 P.M. Monday–Friday and at 9 A.M., 11 A.M., 1 P.M., and 3 P.M. on Saturday, Sunday, and most holidays. Reservations are required for groups of 10 or more and recommended for smaller parties. A welcome center in the East Wing is open 8:30 A.M.–4:30 P.M. Monday–Friday. Its interactive exhibits explain how laws are made. Visitors who call Pennsylvania home can learn about their local legislators and even leave them messages.

Other Harrisburg Sights

The **Broad Street Market** (1233 N. 3rd St., Harrisburg, 717/236-7923, www.broadstreet market.org, 7 A.M.–2 P.M. Wed. with limited

the Pennsylvania State Capitol

© HERSHEYHARRISBURG.ORG

vendors, 7 A.M.–5 P.M. Thurs.–Fri., 7 A.M.–4 P.M. Sat.) is said to be the oldest continuously operating farmers market in the country. Founded in 1860, it's the sole survivor of six markets that once operated in the city. At its peak in the 1920s, the market just a few blocks north of the State Capitol had more than 725 vendors, many of whom leased space outside and waited years for an indoor stall. Today it has about 40 vendors. They hawk everything from hand-rolled soft pretzels to home decor.

One mile north of the Capitol, the **Pennsylvania National Fire Museum** (1820 N. 4th St., Harrisburg, 717/232-8915, www .pnfm.org, 10 A.M.–4 P.M. Tues.–Sat., 1–4 P.M. Sun., admission $6, seniors $5, students $4, family $20) has fascinating answers to questions you may not have thought to ask. Why were firehouses built with spiral staircases? To keep the horses from climbing them. Why the poles? Because spiral staircases slowed down the firemen. Housed in an 1899 Victorian firehouse, the museum traces the history of firefighting from the days of hand-drawn equipment to modern times.

A mile south of the Capitol is **Tröegs**

Brewing Company (800 Paxton St., Harrisburg, 717/232-1297, www.troegs.com, tasting room and gift shop 10 A.M.–5 P.M. Mon.–Fri., noon–4 P.M. Sat.), established in 1997 by brothers Chris and John Trogner. The natives of nearby Mechanicsburg now distribute their beers not only in Pennsylvania but also in half a dozen other states and Washington, D.C. Tours of the brewery behind such frothy delights as HopBack Amber Ale, Troegenator Double Bock, and the seasonal Mad Elf Ale are offered at 1:30, 2, and 2:30 P.M. on Saturdays and usually last 30–40 minutes. Call to reserve spaces. You can samples the goods any day but Sunday. The tasting room is the only place to get your hands on so-called scratch beers, brewed in very small batches using nontraditional ingredients and techniques.

Lake Tobias Wildlife Park

A little drool never hurt anyone. Bear that in mind as elk, oxen, llamas, and other beasts approach you for a snack at Lake Tobias Wildlife Park (760 Tobias Dr., Halifax, 717/362-9126, www.laketobias.com, 10 A.M.–7 P.M. Sat.–Sun. May–Sept., 10 A.M.–6 P.M. Mon.–Fri. and

© HERSHEYHARRISBURG.ORG

Lake Tobias Wildlife Park

10 A.M.–7 P.M. Sat.–Sun. Memorial Day–Labor Day, 10 A.M.–6 P.M. Sat.–Sun. Oct., zoo admission $4, safari tour $5, children under 3 free), about 20 miles north of Harrisburg off Route 225. Africa it's not, but the family-owned animal park offers a safari experience that visitors aren't soon to forget. Specially designed safari cruisers—think school buses with their top halves hacked off—ply 150 rolling acres home to some 500 animals. Among them are species rarely seen in these parts, including water buffalo, the ostrich-like rhea, and the zonkey, a zebra-donkey hybrid. The last safari tour departs one hour before closing. Come too late and you can still have a close encounter with residents of the petting zoo, which include African pygmy goats, Patagonian cavies, armadillos, green monkeys, lemurs, and spotted sheep. Not-so-petable creatures such as lions, tigers, and bears are exhibited in a zoo-like setting. Anacondas, pythons, snapping turtles, and other reptiles entertain company from Memorial Day weekend through Labor Day. Admission to the reptile building is an extra $1.

Millersburg Ferry and Ned Smith Center

Before bridges spanned the Susquehanna River, people and goods crossed it by ferry. John Harris, the first European to permanently settle in the wilderness that would later become Harrisburg, established the first ferry across the river. It became so popular that settlers began referring to the area not by its Indian name but as Harris's Ferry. Today more than 200 bridges stretch across the Susquehanna, which winds its way south from New York to the Chesapeake Bay, and ferry operations are all but extinct. One survives. Now a nostalgic tourist attraction more than anything else, the Millersburg Ferry (717/692-2442, www.millersburg.com, May–Oct. as water conditions allow, one-way walk-on fare $2, autos $6) began shuttling people, produce, livestock, building materials, and more across a mile-wide section of the Susquehanna in the early 1800s. Traffic was heavy enough to keep four boats busy in the early decades of the 20th century. Today the fleet consists of two wooden paddleboats that can accommodate four vehicles and 50 passengers. The ferry connects the quaint town of Millersburg, about 25 miles north of Harrisburg, to a modern campground (32 Ferry Ln., Liverpool, 717/444-3200, www.ferryboatcampsites.com, campsites $22–43, cabins and cottages $45–95) on the west bank of the river. It operates 9 A.M.–dusk on weekends from May through October, plus 11 A.M.–5 P.M. on weekdays from June through Labor Day. To reach the Millersburg landing from Harrisburg, take U.S. 22/322 west to Route 147 north. Follow 147 into Millersburg and turn left onto North Street.

Just outside Millersburg is the **Ned Smith Center for Nature and Art** (176 Water Company Rd., Millersburg, 717/692-3699, www.nedsmithcenter.org, gallery and gift shop 10 A.M.–4 P.M. Tues.–Sat. year-round and noon–4 P.M. Sun. Memorial Day–Labor Day, gallery admission $5, seniors and children 12–18 $2), which celebrates the life and works of a local boy turned nationally recognized wildlife artist. Ned Smith (1919–1985) painted almost 120 covers for the Pennsylvania Game Commission's magazine, created the state's first duck stamp, and illustrated 14 books. Original paintings now command upwards of $60,000. Home to a $1.5 million collection of paintings, drawings, field sketches, journal notes, and manuscripts donated by Smith's widow, the center sits on 500 rustic acres crisscrossed by more than 12 miles of trails. Its gallery showcases the work of contemporary artists and photographers, along with selections from the collection. An outdoor amphitheater is in the works.

ENTERTAINMENT AND EVENTS
Performing Arts

The 600-plus seat **Sunoco Performance Theater** within the Whitaker Center for Science and the Arts (222 Market St., Harrisburg, 717/214-2787, www.whitakercenter.org) hosts live theater, music, and dance by touring and local performers. Resident companies include **Theatre Harrisburg** (717/232-5501, www.theatreharrisburg.com), a community theater

CARLISLE: CAR SHOW CAPITAL

If you love cars, you'll love Carlisle. The Cumberland County seat, about 20 miles southwest of Harrisburg, is named for a town in England, and locals usually emphasize its second syllable. But auto aficionados can't be blamed for thinking the "car" in "Carlisle" has something to do with engines and chrome. The town is the site of collector car, truck, and motorcycle events every season but winter.

Carlisle Events (1000 Bryn Mawr Rd., Carlisle, 717/243-7855, www.carlisleevents.com) rented the Carlisle Fairgrounds when it began producing car shows in the mid-1970s. By 1981 the gatherings had grown so popular that the company purchased the property. Today it hosts 10 annual events. Held in April, **Spring Carlisle** is the kickoff to the season and one of the largest automotive swap meets in the world. **Fall Carlisle**, which caps the season, is another opportunity to buy, sell, and celebrate all things automotive. A car auction is held in conjunction with both events. Between them are specialty shows for Corvettes, Fords, GMs, Chryslers, trucks, motorcycles, imports, and tricked-out "performance and style" vehicles. Visit the Carlisle Events website for a complete schedule, admission fees, and more information.

Car enthusiasts have even more reasons to love Cumberland County. Mechanicsburg, 10 miles east of Carlisle, is home to the **Rolls-Royce Foundation** (189 Hempt Rd., Mechanicsburg, 717/795-9400, www.rollsroycefoundation.com), which operates a research library and museum dedicated to Rolls-Royces and Bentleys. It's open to the public 10 A.M.-2 P.M. Tuesday, Wednesday, and Thursday. Mechanicsburg — named for the mechanics of an earlier vehicle make, the Conestoga wagon — also has an automobile racetrack that dates to 1939. Motorsports legends including Ted Horn, A. J. Foyt, and Mario Andretti have raced at the **Williams Grove Speedway** (1 Speedway Dr., Mechanicsburg, 717/697-5000, www.williamsgrove.com). The half-mile speedway hosts weekly sprint car races from February or March through October. Two other racetracks are within a half-hour drive: the **Quarter Aces Drag-O-Way** (1107 Petersburg Rd., Boiling Springs, 717/258-6287, www.quarteracesdragway.com) and the **Shippensburg Speedway** (178 Walnut Bottom Rd., Shippensburg, 717/532-8581, www.shippensburgspeedway.com).

© JOHN LLOYD

A 1958 Rambler is displayed at the 2010 Fall Carlisle.

that dates to 1926, and the **Harrisburg Choral Society** (877/663-4279, www.harrisburg choralsociety.org), which is even older.

Part of the Capitol Complex, **The Forum** (N. 5th and Walnut Streets, Harrisburg, 717/783-9100) is a 1,763-seat concert hall where "star-studded" refers to the architecture as well as some performances. Its ceiling is studded with hundreds of lights of varying levels of brilliance, arranged to depict constellations. Dedicated in 1931, The Forum is home to the **Harrisburg Symphony Orchestra** (717/545-5527, www.harrisburgsymphony.org).

A storm blew the roof off the **Allenberry Playhouse** (1559 Boiling Springs Rd., Boiling Springs, 717/258-3211, www.allenberry.com) during its dedication in 1949. Adhering to the adage that "the show must go on," the theater didn't let a soaked stage get in the way of its 10-week opening season. Today the season lasts more than 40 weeks, starting in March and running through December. The playhouse on the grounds of Allenberry Resort, about 20 miles southwest of Harrisburg, stages musicals, comedies, and dramas with professional actors. Alumni include John Travolta, who sang and danced on the Allenberry stage in 1971, and Norman Fell, best known for his role as Mr. Roper on *Three's Company*. Allenberry guests are part of the cast during "murder mystery weekends," held October–April.

Festivals and Events

Harrisburg kicks off each year with the largest indoor agricultural event in the nation, the **Pennsylvania Farm Show** (717/787-2905 during show, www.farmshow.state.pa.us, Jan., free). Some 6,000 animals and hundreds of thousands of people pass through the Pennsylvania Farm Show Complex & Expo Center (N. Cameron and Maclay Streets, Harrisburg, 717/787-5373, www.pa-farmshowcomplex.com) during the weeklong event. Farmers from across the state show off the fruits of their labors—everything from pecans to powerful Percherons—in the hopes of taking home prize money and bragging rights. Come for an education in the state's number

one industry, and come on an empty stomach. The Farm Show's best feature could very well be its food court, where a baked potato isn't a humdrum side but a tour de force. Food purchases feed the coffers of nonprofit commodity organizations like Pennsylvania Co-Operative Potato Growers Inc. and the Pennsylvania Maple Syrup Producers Council. Celebrity chefs and culinary students conduct cooking demonstrations using Pennsylvania-grown products. Though admission to the Farm Show is free, parking isn't.

Come February, hunting and fishing enthusiasts pack the Farm Show Complex. The **Eastern Sports & Outdoor Show** (800/467-5656, www .easternsportshow.com, admission charged) is a chance for them to check out the newest gear, chat up professional outdoorsmen, book excursions with top guides, and shop for boats, RVs, ATVs, and other cool rides. It's the largest consumer event of its kind in North America.

Harrisburg's largest arts event is the **Patriot-News Artsfest** (717/238-5180, www.harris burgarts.org, Memorial Day weekend). Named one of the top 100 arts events in the country by *Sunshine Artist* magazine, Artsfest brings some 275 artists and craftspeople from around the country to Riverfront Park. Music lovers have as much reason to turn out as art lovers: Free concerts are a festival staple. The Whitaker Center for Science and the Arts hosts an independent film festival in conjunction with Artsfest.

Live music—sans cover charge—is a hallmark of summers in Harrisburg. The city's Department of Parks & Recreation sponsors two outdoor entertainment series. On Saturdays young and old congregate around Reservoir Park's restored 1940s-era bandshell for the latest installment of the **Levitt Live!** (717/255-3020, www.levittlive.com, June–Aug.) series. The genre? Might be classical. Might be reggae. Might be Shakespeare or spoken word. Check the website for the lineup. Reservoir Park, the city's largest park and the site of the National Civil War Museum, is on the eastern end of the city, reachable from downtown by both State and Market Streets. The bandshell is near the entrance at State and 20th Streets.

On Sunday evenings the action shifts to Italian Lake, a diminutive park at Third and Division Streets in the neighborhood known as Uptown. The **Italian Lake Concert Series** (717/255-3020, www.harrisburgevents.com, July–Aug.) brings folk, classical, jazz, and world music to the masses. The masses bring lawn chairs, blankets, and refreshments.

The city marks Independence Day and Labor Day with free festivals in Riverfront Park. Held over July 4 weekend, the **Harrisburg Jazz and Multi-Cultural Festival** attracts gobs of local, regional, and national musicians. There's plenty to keep kids occupied, including amusement rides and video karaoke. A spectacular fireworks display caps three days of virtually uninterrupted music. **Kipona,** held over Labor Day weekend, is Harrisburg's annual homage to the Susquehanna River. (Kipona means "bright, sparkling water" in the Delaware Indian tongue.) It's a blockbuster of a festival. You've got all the fixings of the Jazz and Multi-Cultural Festival: live entertainment on multiple stages, children's activities, fireworks, food, and more food. You've also got a chili cook-off—not just any chili cook-off but the Pennsylvania State Chili Cook-Off (www.chiefchili.com), a qualifying event for the International Chili Society's world championship. The competition is, um, hot. Adding hilarity to the so-called Chili Bowl are eating contests open to the public. Cash, hot sauces, and sympathy go to the man or woman who eats the most jalapenos in 60 seconds. The perennial festival is also the occasion for a Native American encampment on City Island. The powwow, as it's called, features demonstrations of traditional dance, drumming, and arts and crafts. Elk jerky and sassafras tea are on offer. Some 150 artists and craftspeople from around the country sell their works at the southern end of Riverfront Park. There's a fee for admission to the arts area. Other Kipona traditions include canoe races, a bass fishing tournament, a youth street soccer competition, and a karate tournament. Visit the website of the Department of Parks & Recreation, www.harrisburgevents.com, or call 717/255-3020

for more information about Kipona or the Jazz and Multi-Cultural Festival.

SPORTS AND RECREATION
City Island
Harrisburg's recreational hub is a 63-acre city park surrounded by water. The mid-river City Island (717/255-3020, www.harrisburgevents.com) boasts a beach, sand volleyball courts, a multipurpose field, a playground, picnic pavilions, and three marinas. If you don't have a boat of your own, board the **Pride of the Susquehanna** (717/234-6500, www.harrisburgriverboat.com), an old-fashioned paddlewheeler that plies the river May–October. Alternatively, set off in a kayak or canoe from **Susquehanna Outfitters** (717/503-0066, www.susquehannaoutfitters.com, 10 A.M.–6 P.M. Sat.–Sun., weekdays by reservation), which also rents bicycles. Work on your swing on an elaborate 18-hole miniature golf course (717/232-8533) or in the batting cages. Catch pros in action at Metro Bank Park, home to Harrisburg's minor league baseball team (717/231-4444, www.senatorsbaseball.com). Other City Island attractions include an antique carousel and scaled-down versions of a Civil War–era steam train and San Francisco–style trolley.

You can walk or bike to the island from downtown Harrisburg via the Walnut Street Bridge, which was closed to cars after Hurricane Agnes in 1972 and lost some of its western spans in 1996 flooding. Cars access the island via the Market Street Bridge, a stone arch bridge spanning the Susquehanna.

Riverfront Park and Capital Area Greenbelt
After-church strolls through Riverfront Park were de rigueur for Harrisburg's middle and upper classes in the early 1900s. No need to wear your Sunday best for a visit to the 4.5-mile ribbon of lawns and gardens along the Susquehanna, often co-opted for festivals, runs and walks, weddings, and other special events. Stretching from Vine Street up to Vaughn Street, the lush park is punctuated by public art, picnic

tables, benches, and plazas. Paved paths make it ideal not just for strolling but also for inline skating and biking. Riverfront Park is part of the 20-mile Capital Area Greenbelt (717/921-4733, www.caga.org), a mostly paved, mostly car-free recreational route. Rental bikes of all sizes are available at City Island's **Susquehanna Outfitters** (717/503-0066, www.susquehanna outfitters.com, 10 A.M.–6 P.M. Sat.–Sun., weekdays by reservation).

Appalachian Trail

The **Appalachian Trail Conservancy** (304/535-6331, www.appalachiantrail.org),

the volunteer-based organization charged with managing and protecting the famous footpath, has an information center about 15 miles southwest of Harrisburg. The center (4 E. 1st St., Boiling Springs, 717/258-5771) is staffed 8 A.M.–3:30 P.M. weekdays year-round. You can get answers to questions about short jaunts, thru-hikes, and everything in between, plus guidebooks, maps, postcards, and A.T. merchandise. It's not unusual to find volunteers doling out information on the front porch on summer weekends.

The A.T. crosses the Susquehanna River at Duncannon, about 15 miles north of the

A MYRIAD OF MINOR LEAGUE TEAMS

Harrisburg doesn't have a single major league franchise, but its sports fans have plenty to cheer about. The Hershey-Harrisburg region has so many professional and semi-pro teams that Street & Smith's *SportsBusiness Journal* named it the nation's top minor league market in 2009. Best known of Harrisburg's franchises is the **Harrisburg Senators** (Metro Bank Park, City Island, Harrisburg, 717/231-4444, www.senatorsbaseball.com), the Class AA affiliate of the Washington Nationals. Formed in 1987, the baseball team won the Eastern League championship in its first season. It won four consecutive championships from 1996 to 1999, becoming the first team in league history to do so. More than 200 of its players have been called up to the majors.

Football fans have a host of teams to watch, including the **Harrisburg Stampede** (717/889-0344, www.harrisburgstampede.com), a 2009 expansion team in the American Indoor Football Association. Home games are held at the Pennsylvania Farm Show Complex & Expo Center (N. Cameron and Maclay Streets, Harrisburg, 717/787-5373, www.pafarmshowcomplex.com), which also hosts the state's annual livestock show – hence the team's name. The season runs from March through June. Harrisburg is also home to two members of the North American Football League: the **Central Penn Piranha** (www.eteamz.com/piranhafootball), which bills

itself as the "winningest team in minor league football history," and the **South Central Yard Dawgs** (www.htosports.com/?djohnson). Their regular season begins in July. Then there's women's full-contact football. The **Central PA Vipers** (www.centralpavipers.com) of the Independent Women's Football League compete for talent with Harrisburg's other women's team, the **Keystone Assault** (717/222-8570, www.keystoneassault.com) of the Women's Football Alliance. Both leagues have 10-week seasons beginning in April.

Harrisburg has something for basketball and soccer fans, too. The **Harrisburg Horizon** (717/986-0499, www.harrisburghorizon.com) won seven consecutive Eastern Basketball Alliance championships from 2002 to 2008. The league's season begins in December and ends in March. The **City Islanders** (717/441-4625, www.cityislanders.com), members of the United Soccer Leagues Second Division, play home games at Skyline Sports Complex, next to Metro Bank Park on City Island. Their season kicks off in April.

The city's hockey fans needn't go far to catch action on ice. In 2009 the **Hershey Bears** (Giant Center, 550 W. Hersheypark Dr., Hershey, 717/508-2327, www.hersheybears.com) became the first team in American Hockey League history to clinch 10 championships.

state capital. Duncannon's **Doyle Hotel** (7 N. Market St., 717/834-6789, www.doylehotel .com) is a legendary stop along the Georgia-to-Maine trail. It's a bit of a dive, but that's part of its charm. The hotel serves food and drink, accepts mail drops, and plasters its walls with photos of thru-hikers. Rooms are $25 per night, and Internet service is free to hikers.

Water Activities

Almost a mile wide at Harrisburg, the Susquehanna River tempts outdoor lovers to float or fish the day away. Among the enablers: **Susquehanna Outfitters** (main parking lot of City Island, 717/503-0066, www.susque hannaoutfitters.com, 10 A.M.–6 P.M. Sat.–Sun., weekdays by reservation, half-day boat rental $39–49, full-day boat rental $52–62, 2-hour bicycle rental $10) with its rental fleet of river canoes and sit-on-top kayaks. Paddlers are shuttled to one of two put-ins upstream, from which they make their back to the outfitter's base on City Island. Paddling is hardly necessary. If you're feeling lazy, the south-flowing Susquehanna will do most of the work for you. Boat rental rates include basic instruction, life jackets, and the shuttle, which departs every two hours 10 A.M.–4 P.M. on weekends and by reservation on weekdays, weather permitting. Paddlers with boats of their own can hitch a ride for $7–10. Susquehanna Outfitters is owned by a local husband and wife who are happy to point you to prime swimming, fishing, and picnicking spots on the island-studded river. They also offer guided tours.

If you want to paddle for days, fishing in secluded coves and sleeping in riverfront campgrounds or primitive island campsites, you want to call **Blue Mountain Outfitters** (U.S. 11/15, 2 miles north of I-81 interchange, Marysville, 717/957-2413, www.bluemountainoutfitters .net, 10 A.M.–8 P.M. Tues., 10 A.M.–6 P.M. Wed.–Sat., open Sun. in warmer months, 1-day boat rental $45–65, each additional day $35–55, reservations recommended). Located several miles north of Harrisburg on the west side of the Susquehanna, Blue Mountain is a full-service paddle sports store with a wide

selection of canoes, kayaks, and accessories. It also sells some camping gear. During the warmer months, it rents canoes, one- and two-person recreational kayaks, and one-person touring kayaks. Paddlers can start at Blue Mountain and float downstream or hop on a shuttle to explore the river's more northerly stretches. The outfitter, housed in an erstwhile train station, offers lifts to put-ins upwards of 40 miles away for multi-day trips. It also facilitates trips on the Juniata River, Sherman Creek, and other nearby waterways when water levels permit. Rental rates don't include shuttle services, which are also available for privately owned boats. Novice paddlers and shutterbugs can leave the piloting to Blue Mountain's pros by booking a trip on the "war canoe"—a 22-foot vessel that can accommodate eight people. The ride is especially thrilling during high water.

The Harrisburg-area section of the Susquehanna is a top-notch smallmouth bass fishery. Anglers can also get bites from catfish, carp, panfish, and other swimmers. Short on poppers, plastic crayfish, or rubber worms? No worries. Harrisburg Mall is home to Pennsylvania's only **Bass Pro Shops** (3501 Paxton St., Harrisburg, 717/565-5200, www.basspro.com, 9 A.M.–9 P.M. Mon.–Sat., 10 A.M.–6 P.M. Sun.). The mammoth store is as much a spiritual experience as shopping experience for fishing and hunting fanatics. With its 60,000-gallon aquarium and wildlife dioramas, it's also a family attraction. The store boasts a rock-climbing wall, a NASCAR simulator, an archery range, and a boat showroom.

Yellow Breeches Creek, which flows through communities to Harrisburg's southwest and dumps into the Susquehanna three miles south of City Island, is among the most popular trout streams in the state. Anglers interested in the stocking program can visit the **Huntsdale State Fish Hatchery** (195 Lebo Rd. in the village of Huntsdale, 12 miles southwest of Carlisle, 717/486-3419, www.fish.state .pa.us, visitor center 8 A.M.–3:30 P.M. daily), which produces brook trout, brown trout, rainbow trout, and golden rainbow trout, along with striped bass, channel catfish, and tiger muskellunge. Fly fishers flock to a mile-long catch-and-release section in the town of Boiling Springs, which has an excellent fly shop, **Yellow Breeches Outfitters** (2 First St., Boiling Springs, 717/258-6752, www.yellow breeches.com, regular season 9 A.M.–5 P.M. Tues.–Thurs., 9 A.M.–6 P.M. Fri., 9 A.M.–5 P.M. Sat., 9 A.M.–4 P.M. Sun., open only Fri.–Sun. in winter). The shop sells a wide variety of rods, reels, waders, and other gear from England-based Hardy & Greys. Other products include Echo rods, Beulah rods, and Patagonia clothing and gear. It offers fly-fishing instruction and guided fishing on the Yellow Breeches, Letort Spring Run, and other fabled streams in the area. Smallmouth guiding on the Susquehanna is also available. A full day with an experienced guide is $250 for one angler, $375 for two. **Allenberry Resort Inn and Playhouse** (1559 Boiling Springs Rd., Boiling Springs, 717/258-3211, www.allenberry.com), at the downstream end of the no-kill area, offers fly-fishing courses on select weekends.

ACCOMMODATIONS

If you're looking for a central location, look no further than the **(Hilton Harrisburg** (1 N. 2nd St., Harrisburg, 717/233-6000, www .hilton.com, $112–239). Just three blocks from the State Capitol Complex and the bridges to City Island, the hotel is connected via an enclosed walkway to the Whitaker Center for Science and the Arts and a shopping center called Strawberry Square. Its 300-plus guest rooms and suites are outfitted with flat-panel TVs, refrigerators, coffee makers, and Hilton's trademark Serenity beds. Guests of Executive Level rooms have access to a private lounge where a complimentary continental breakfast and evening hors d'oeuvres are served. All guests get free wireless Internet access and weekday *USA Today* newspapers. The hotel is at the end of Harrisburg's Restaurant Row, but finding an excellent meal is easier than stepping outside. The Hilton is home the **The Golden Sheaf** (717/237-6400, lunch for hotel guests 11 A.M.–2 P.M. Mon.–Fri., dinner 5:30–10 P.M.

Mon.–Sat., lunch $10–17, dinner $28–48), the city's only AAA Four Diamond restaurant. Its casual restaurant, **Raspberries** (717/237-6419, breakfast 6:30–11 A.M. Mon.–Fri., 7 A.M.–1 P.M. Sat., and 7–11 A.M. Sun., brunch 11 A.M.–2 P.M. Sun., lunch 11:30 A.M.–2 P.M. Mon.–Fri., dinner 5–10 P.M. daily, $10–24), is best known for its outstanding Sunday brunch, set to live music.

Nestled on the west shore of the Susquehanna River, **Bridgeview Bed & Breakfast** (810 S. Main St., Marysville, 717/957-2438, www .bridgeviewbnb.com, single occupancy $100–110, double occupancy $120–130, triple occupancy $160, weeknights $80–120) doesn't have antique furnishings, luxury linens, heaven-scented bath products, or even in-room televisions. Breakfast isn't what you'd call gourmet. It does have killer views of the river and the Rockville Bridge, famous for being the world's longest stone masonry arch railroad bridge. Built in the opening years of the 20th century by the Pennsylvania Railroad, the bridge still sees a good deal of train traffic—which makes the Bridgeview a magnet for train buffs. The B&B, formerly a sporting goods and tackle shop, has 10 en suite guest rooms, three of which have private entrances from outside. The rooms are named for Pennsylvania's great rivers. Fittingly enough, the Susquehanna Room is the largest and most expensive.

FOOD

Pennsylvania's politicos don't have to venture far from the Capitol Complex to strategize or negotiate over a meal that receives bipartisan approval. The strip known as Restaurant Row is a stone's throw away. Roughly defined as the section of 2nd Street between Market and State Streets, Restaurant Row has eateries both casual and upscale, American and ethnic. Consider walking its length before settling on a choice. One you won't regret: **(Café Fresco** (215 N. 2nd St., Harrisburg, 717/236-2599, www.cafefresco.com, 7 A.M.–11 P.M. Mon.–Wed., 7 A.M.–1 A.M. Thurs.–Sat., $4–41). By day, it's a chic but casual spot, offering breakfast items for under $5, sandwiches on rolls or homemade flat bread, wraps, burgers, salads, and pizzas. It glams up in the evening, becoming a destination for swishy cocktails and high-end, Asian-influenced cuisine, though casual fare such as pizzas and a Kobe burger are still on offer. After dinner, you can sashay upstairs to get your groove on. At **Level 2** (717/236-6600, www.level2.us, 8 P.M.–2 A.M. Thurs.–Sat.), one of a handful of nightlife spots in the state capital, the dress code is "fashionable and fierce," and the DJs are tireless. Bottle service is available. For those who come hungry, there's a menu of small plates courtesy of Café Fresco's chef.

If it's Motown or jazz that brings you to the dance floor, show up at **Stock's on 2nd** (211 N. 2nd St., Harrisburg, 717/233-6699, www .stocksonsecond.com, lunch from 11:30 A.M. Mon.–Fri., dinner from 5 P.M. daily, $9–30) on a Saturday night. The music begins at 9:30 P.M., and there's never a cover charge. Another excellent time to visit Stock's: 5–7 P.M. on a weekday. That's when select draft beers are $1, single-liquor well drinks are $2, and everything on the bar and lounge menu is half price. (Don't think typical bar fare. Think lamb sliders, roasted tomato and basil bisque, and chips made from beets as well as tubers.) The restaurant's lunch and dinner menus are also mouthwatering, with crab cakes and Delmonico steak among the specialties. An exhibition kitchen and oversized Leroy Neiman artwork lend to the lighthearted atmosphere. So do the generous martinis.

Ethnic options on Restaurant Row include **Miyako Sushi on Second** (227 N. 2nd St., Harrisburg, 717/234-3250, 11 A.M.–10 P.M. Mon.–Thurs., 11 A.M.–11 P.M. Fri., noon–11 P.M. Sat., $5–19), which offers Japanese-style omelets and casseroles, a variety of teriyaki platters, and udon and soba noodle dishes as well as sushi.

Third Street is home to the *muy excelente* **El Sol Mexican Restaurant** (18 S. 3rd St., Harrisburg, 717/901-5050, www.elsolmexican restaurant.net, 11 A.M.–10 P.M. Mon.–Thurs., 11 A.M.–11 P.M. Fri., 4–11 P.M. Sat., $7–24). Owners Juan and Lisa Garcia—he

of the Guadalajara region of Mexico, she of Harrisburg—specialize in dishes from his home state, but they pull off burritos, fajitas, and other familiar fare with equal aplomb. The ceviche, made with tilapia, is an excellent appetizer. Popular entrées include *camarones a la diabla* (shrimp and mushrooms sautéed in a spicy sauce) and *bistek Guadalajara* (steak topped with sautéed vegetables and cheese). Also outstanding are the *molcajetes*—medleys of meat and/or seafood served in the Mexican version of a mortar. All sauces are made from scratch, and customers can dictate the level of spiciness. El Sol also makes its own Mexican beverages, including a sweetened rice drink known as horchata and fresh-squeezed limeade. For those who want something harder, there's beer and a tequila selection unmatched in Harrisburg. Try a tequila flight if you're new to the Mexican liquor.

Across the street at **B Bricco** (31 S. 3rd St., Harrisburg, 717/724-0222, www.bricco pa.com, lunch 11:30 A.M.–2:30 P.M. Mon.–Fri., dinner 5:30–10 P.M. Mon.–Sat. and 4:30–10 P.M. Sun., $8–34), executive chef Jason Viscount creates masterly Mediterranean dishes with the help of students from the Olewine School of Culinary Arts at Harrisburg Area Community College. Though inspired by Tuscan cuisine, Bricco sources Pennsylvania products whenever possible. Particularly popular are its raw-bar offerings and pizzas, baked in a stone oven and topped with delicacies such as fig jam, white truffle oil, and local feta. The restaurant, a collaboration between the Olewine School and the managing general partner of the Hilton Harrisburg, boasts an extensive wine list—about 50 varieties by the glass and well over 200 by the bottle. Wine enthusiasts have the opportunity to sample three for $12–16. Formaggi, or cheeses, have a menu of their own. Fall in love with one and you can buy some to take home at **Olewine's Meat and Cheese House** (306 Chestnut St., Harrisburg, 717/724-0246, 11 A.M.–5 P.M. Tues.–Fri., 10 A.M.–2 P.M. Sat.). Located around the corner from Bricco, the shop also sells a wide variety of hand-cut meats, fresh seafood, and deli sandwiches. Bricco's bakery, **Ciao!** (304 Chestnut St., Harrisburg, 717/724-0236, 6:30 A.M.–4 P.M. Mon.–Fri.) carries artisan breads, breakfast pastries, and desserts.

Housed in a restored 1871 firehouse, **Fire House** (606 N. 2nd St., Harrisburg, 717/234-6064, www.thefirehouserestaurant .com, 11:30 A.M.–10 P.M. Mon.–Thurs., 11:30 A.M.–11 P.M. Fri.–Sat., 4–9 P.M. Sun., $6–35) is worth a visit if only to watch beer pour from a fire hydrant. Food's good, too. Highly regarded for its prime rib, slow-roasted every evening, and baby-back ribs, the casual American eatery also finds a place for pork on its appetizer list. "Pork wings," we're told, are twice the size of hot wings and healthier to boot. The multi-level restaurant's Maryland-style crab cakes are phenomenal, either as an entrée with sweet potato fries or atop a salad.

INFORMATION

The **Hershey Harrisburg Regional Visitors Bureau** (17 S. 2nd St., Harrisburg, 717/231-7788, www.hersheyharrisburg.org, 9 A.M.–5 P.M. Mon.–Fri. and 10 A.M.–3 P.M. Sat., also open 10 A.M.–2 P.M. Sun. in summer) is a good source of information about attractions, lodging, and dining in and around the state capital. Visit the bureau's website to request a copy of its current visitors guide or peruse a digital version.

GETTING THERE AND AROUND

Harrisburg is about 15 miles west of Hershey and 40 miles northwest of Lancaster. **Harrisburg International Airport** (888/235-9442, www .flyhia.com) is served by Air Canada, AirTran Airways, Continental Airlines, Delta Air Lines, United Airlines, and US Airways. They offer daily nonstop service to about a dozen destinations. Note that while locals refer to the airport as HIA, its Federal Aviation Administration booking code is MDT. That's because of its physical location in the borough of Middletown, about eight miles south of Harrisburg.

The Harrisburg Transportation Center, located at 4th and Chestnut Streets, is served by **Amtrak** (800/872-7245, www.amtrak .com), **Greyhound** (800/231-2222, www.grey hound.com), and other intercity bus operators. Local bus services are provided by **Capital Area Transit** (717/238-8304, www.cattransit .com). The base fare is $1.65 for adults, $1.15 for students. Transfers are $0.25. Bus drivers don't make change. Multiple-ride tickets and monthly passes can be purchased at CAT's main office (901 N. Cameron St., Harrisburg, 7:30 A.M.–4:30 P.M. Mon.–Fri., 9 A.M.–1 P.M. last Sat. of every month) and at kiosks in locations including Strawberry Square shopping center (2nd and Market Streets, Harrisburg, 10 A.M.–6 P.M. Mon.–Fri., 10 A.M.–5 P.M. Sat.). They're also available through CAT's website.

York County

Just west of Lancaster County, York County touts itself as the "Factory Tour Capital of the World." Indeed, about a dozen factories open their doors to visitors. Frugal families can live it up here; admission is free in almost every case. So many of the factories are dedicated to guilty pleasures that York County also claims the title of Snack Food Capital of the World. I know what you're thinking: York Peppermint Patties. Alas, the brand born here in 1940 now belongs to Hershey Co., and the minty, chocolatey confections are made elsewhere. But

York County is home to another candy company, potato chip makers Martin's and Utz, and pretzel producer Snyder's of Hanover. The biggest name on the factory circuit has nothing to do with mmmm-mmmm and everything to do with vroom-vroom. Harley-Davidson's York operations attract bikers from across the United States and countries as far-flung as Turkey, China, and Australia.

In recent years, York County has strived to make a name for itself in wine circles. The ranks of the UnCork York Wine Trail swelled

© WWW.YORKPA.ORG

York County is home to the potato chip maker Martin's.

to 13 family-owned wineries in 2009. Napa it's not, but boosters cast that as a virtue. Because the area's wineries are modest operations, visitors can count on face time with people close to the winemaking process—often the owners themselves.

Long before the county became the Factory Tour Capital, its only city, also named York, served as the capital of what would soon be known as the United States of America. The Continental Congress, that body of delegates who spoke for the colonies during the Revolutionary period, met in York for nine months in 1777 and 1778, adopting the Articles of Confederation. The York County Heritage Trust operates several museums and historic sites that offer a window into the past. Murals throughout downtown York also serve as a record of local history.

The county's greatest asset could be its location in the center of Pennsylvania Dutch Country. Gettysburg and its Civil War battlefield are 30 miles west of York. Lancaster's Amish farmlands are about that distance to its

east. The state capital, Harrisburg, is 25 miles north of the city, and Hershey, a.k.a. "The Sweetest Place on Earth," is just 10 miles farther. That makes York County a good base of operations for travelers who want to take in the more touristy areas without paying touristy lodging prices.

FACTORY TOURS

The Factory Tour Capital of the World has more factories than you can visit in a day—or even two—so making your picks is job one. You'll find a complete list of factory tours at www.yorkpa.org, the website of the York County Convention & Visitors Bureau. Not to be missed is **Wolfgang Candy Company** (50 E. 4th Ave., York, 800/248-4273, www .wolfgangcandy.com, walk-in tours on the hour 10 A.M.–2 P.M. Mon.–Thurs. in summer, call or check website for fall–spring schedule, store and museum open 8 A.M.–4:30 P.M. Mon.–Fri. and 10 A.M.–3 P.M. Sat. year-round, free), where you can watch chocolate-covered pretzels, bear-shaped chocolates filled with creamy peanut butter, or other confections take shape. Founded in 1921, the family-owned company still makes chocolate in small batches using vintage equipment. Tours last 45 minutes to an hour and end with free samples. You'll be asked to remove jewelry and don a hairnet (gents with beards or long mustaches get extra nets) before entering production areas. A museum that tells the story of the Wolfgang family's adventure in candy-making and a store, Das Sweeten Haus, are open daily except Sunday. Save room for a milkshake from the old-timey soda fountain.

Less than three miles away is **Harley-Davidson's York Vehicle Operations** (1425 Eden Rd., York, 877/883-1450, www.harley-davidson.com/experience, tours at regular intervals 9 A.M.–2 P.M. Mon.–Fri., tour center and gift shop open 8 A.M.–4 P.M. Mon.–Fri., free). Established in 1973, the motorcycle assembly facility grew into Harley's largest manufacturing site and York County's largest manufacturing employer. But the legendary motorcycle company wasn't immune to the Great Recession of 2009. In mid-year it announced that the York operations, where Touring and Softail models are assembled, were "not currently competitive or sustainable" and that relocating was under consideration. The community breathed a collective sign of relief at the close of the year, when a combination of union concessions and state incentives convinced the company to stay put and scale back. Tours, which last about an hour, begin with a brief movie, continue through various manufacturing and assembly areas, and conclude at the end of the line, where every motorcycle is roll-tested before being crated and shipped. Children under 12 aren't allowed on the factory floor, but they're welcome in the tour center, which includes exhibits about assembly processes and motorcycles for the straddling.

If you head west on U.S. 30 from Harley, you'll reach **Martin's Potato Chips** (5847 Lincoln Hwy./U.S. 30, Thomasville, 800/272-4477, www.martinschips.com, tours on the hour 9–11 A.M. Tues. by reservation, store open 8:30 A.M.–2:30 P.M. Mon.–Fri., free) in about 15 minutes. But the epicenter of the

touring Harley-Davidson's York Vehicle Operations

county's snack foods industry is the borough of Hanover, about 20 miles southwest of York. That's where you'll find **Snyder's of Hanover** (1350 York St., Hanover, 800/233-7125 ext. 8592, www.snydersofhanover.com, tours 10 A.M., 11 A.M., and 1 P.M. Tues.–Thurs. by reservation, store open 9 A.M.–6 P.M. Mon.–Sat. and noon–5 P.M. Sun., free), best known for its pretzels. Snyder's snacks are sold on every continent except Africa and Antarctica, so tours of the Hanover facilities are an education in large-scale manufacturing. You'll get to see the raw material warehouse, finished goods warehouse, packing room, and oven room. The one-hour tour includes a primer on potato chip making and finishes in the factory store, where you'll get a free bag of pretzels and bargains on everything from Old Tyme Pretzels, first made in 1909, to the popular flavored pretzel pieces, introduced some 80 years later.

At **Utz Quality Foods** (900 High St., Hanover, 800/367-7629, www.utzsnacks.com, self-guided tours 8 A.M.–4 P.M. Mon.–Thurs., call for Fri. hours, free), you can watch raw spuds become crunchy chips from a glass-lined gallery. Though famous for its chips—Rachael Ray talked up Utz Kettle Classics Potato Chips on her eponymous TV show—the company also makes pretzels, cheese curls, pork rinds, and more. Its outlet store (861 Carlisle St., Hanover, 8 A.M.–7 P.M. Mon.–Sat., 11 A.M.–6 P.M. Sun.) is two blocks from the main plant.

Far smaller than Snyder's or Utz, **Revonah Pretzels** (507 Baltimore St., Hanover, 717/630-2883, www.revonahpretzel.com, tours 9:30 A.M.–noon Tues.–Thurs., reservations recommended, free) takes its name from the town (Revonah is Hanover spelled backwards) and its cues from the past. Pretzels are rolled and twisted by hand, hearth-baked, and slowly hardened in a kiln. Word has it that the Pittsburgh Steelers munch on these when they're on the road. Visitors can sample a "greenie," a pretzel that's crunchy on the outside but still warm and soft on the inside.

If it's a warm, sunny day, be sure to include **Perrydell Farm Dairy** (90 Indian Rock Dam Rd., York, 717/741-3485, www.perrydellfarm.com, self-guided tours 7 A.M.–9 P.M.

© WWW.YORKPA.ORG

Pretzels are made by hand at Renovah Pretzels.

Mon.–Sat., noon–6 P.M. Sun., free) on your itinerary. Depending on when you visit the family-owned farm, which eschews artificial growth hormones, you might see cows being milked, calves being fed, or milk being bottled. The oh-so-fresh milk is sold on-site, along with hand-dipped ice cream, locally grown produce, and locally baked goods.

Be sure to wear comfortable, closed-toe shoes when you go factory hopping. Open-toe shoes and heels are prohibited in some areas.

UNCORK YORK WINE TRAIL

Central Pennsylvania's reputation as a wine region is growing, albeit slowly, in part because its wineries are within easy reach of metropolitan areas and in part because of savvy marketing. Even people who don't much care for wine are lured to the wineries by concerts, pig roasts, chances to stomp grapes à la Lucy Ricardo, and other crowd-pleasing programming. One of the happening-est spots in York County is **Moon Dancer Vineyards & Winery** (1282 Klines Run Rd., Wrightsville, 717/252-9463, www .moondancerwinery.com, noon–5 P.M. Wed.– Thurs., noon–9 P.M. Fri., 11 A.M.–6 P.M. Sat.– Sun.). It hosts live music on Fridays, Saturdays, and Sundays year-round and annual jazz, bluegrass, folk, and reggae festivals. In the warmer months, visitors can mingle on the patio or picnic on the grounds of the French chateau–like winery overlooking the Susquehanna River. In the colder ones, they're invited to sip hot mulled wine by a fire.

Of course, winemaking is the primary business of Moon Dancer and other wineries along the UnCork York Wine Trail (www.uncorkyork .com). And they're turning out some high-caliber wines, from sweet wines infused with apples, peaches, and other fruits so plentiful in Pennsylvania to European-style dry wines. Boasts one area winemaker: "California wine tastes like sunshine. Big deal. Mine tastes like earth and the four seasons." The oldest winery in York County, **Naylor Wine Cellars** (4069 Vineyard Rd., Stewartstown, 800/293-3370, www.naylorwine.com, 11 A.M.–6 P.M. Mon.– Sat., noon–5 P.M. Sun.) has collected medals at

© WWW.YORKPA.ORG

Wine that "tastes like earth and the four seasons" can be found along the UnCork York Wine Trail.

statewide and international competitions. Be sure to sample the award-winning Cabernet and the port-style Essence of Chambourcin. Tours of the winery are free and require no advance notice. If you're interested in touring the vineyard with its labrusca, vinifera, and French-American grapes, call ahead to make arrangements. On Saturday evenings in the summer, Naylor hosts dances to big band music. "Wine dinners" draw visitors in the winter.

Allegro Vineyards (3475 Sechrist Rd., Brogue, 717/927-9148, www.allegrowines .com, 1–5 P.M. Wed.–Sun.) grows six varieties of grapes on five acres, including Cabernet Sauvignon and Chardonnay. Founded by musician brothers, Allegro opened to the public in 1981. It's now owned by husband and wife Carl Helrich and Kris Miller, but the wine list is still sprinkled with musical references. There's a dessert wine named Aria, a sparkling wine called Serenade, and the 2005 Cadenza, Allegro's Bordeaux-inspired flagship red. Check the website for a calendar of concerts and other events at the winery and **Allegro Wine Gallery** (2549 S. Queen St., York, 717/741-3072, noon–6 P.M. Sun.–Thurs., noon–8 P.M. Fri., 11 A.M.–7 P.M. Sat.), a shop-cum-gallery in the Olde Tollgate Village shopping center, a few miles south of downtown York.

There's no better time to visit the UnCork York wineries than during **Tour de Tanks,** a celebration of new vintages held weekends in March. A $20 ticket gives you access to the cellars of all participating wineries, where you can taste the season's upcoming wines before they're bottled. Winemakers are on hand to answer questions. Visit the UnCork York website for more information about the event, a complete list of wineries, a downloadable map of the trail, and a list of hotels and B&Bs that offer wine-themed packages.

OTHER SIGHTS
Central Market

York's public market house is a can't-miss if you're in town on a Tuesday, Thursday, or Saturday. Built in 1888, Central Market (34 W. Philadelphia St., York, 717/848-2243, www.centralmarketyork.com, 6 A.M.–2 P.M. Tues., Thurs., and Sat.) is not just a showcase for area farmers but also a hopping lunch spot. In fact, lunch counters outnumber produce stands by more than three to one. You'll find Greek food, Puerto Rican food, and Italian food. You'll find soups and sandwiches at Busy Bee, opened in 2009 by the chef de cuisine of York's exclusive Lafayette Club. Roburrito's, a popular local burrito joint, also joined the vendor ranks in 2009. You can't miss its stand, which resembles a foil-wrapped burrito and serves up venison-stuffed burritos during deer season. Fresh-cut french fries, freshly baked cupcakes, and hot pretzels make it nearly impossible to avoid an indulgence.

York County Heritage Trust

History buffs will be happy to find more than half a dozen museums and historic sites within walking distance of each other in downtown York. Operated by the York County Heritage Trust (250 E. Market St., 717/848-1587,

www.yorkheritage.org), they include the **Agricultural and Industrial Museum** (217 W. Princess St., 10 A.M.–4 P.M. Tues.–Sat.), which houses artifacts spanning three centuries. Its collection includes a 72-ton A-frame ammonia compressor, once used to manufacture large blocks of ice; a three-story gristmill; and locally made tractors and farm tools. Exhibits cover topics as diverse as casket manufacturing, piano and organ manufacturing, and York's industrial contribution to World War II. The 12,000-square-foot transportation wing showcases automobiles made in York, a Conestoga wagon, and a 1937 Aeronca K airplane.

Just two blocks away is the **Colonial Complex** (corner of W. Market St. and N. Pershing Ave., 10 A.M.–4 P.M. Tues.–Sat., closed mid-Dec.–late Mar.), four buildings that transport visitors to earlier times. Among them is the **Golden Plough Tavern,** the oldest structure in town. Built in 1741, it served as a hotel and restaurant and today is furnished with Pennsylvania furniture predating 1760. Adjacent to it is the **General Gates House,** built circa 1751 by the tavern's second owner. It's named for General Horatio Gates, the Revolutionary War hero who lived in the house during York's turn as the de facto capital of the American colonies. In 1777, as Philadelphia fell into the hands of the British, the Continental Congress moved west, spending one day in Lancaster before crossing the Susquehanna River and settling in York on September 30. After Gates defeated the British near Saratoga, New York, the Congress invited him to York, where he was feted and named president of the Board of War. Some members of Congress had bigger plans for him. Unimpressed with General George Washington's command of the Continental Army, they plotted to replace him with Gates. The "Conway Cabal," as the intrigue was dubbed, unraveled when France's Marquis de Lafayette proposed a toast to General Washington during a banquet at the Gates House. Eager for France's support in the war against Britain, the conspirators quit their plotting. Today the house reflects the year—1778—when history was made there.

Across the street from the Gates House and tavern is a reconstruction of the courthouse where Congressional delegates met during their nine-month stay in York. The original courthouse was located two blocks away. Behind the Gates House and tavern is the **Barnett Bobb Log House,** built in the early 1800s and named for its builder, a German immigrant. It's furnished to reflect family life in the 1830s. Tours of the Colonial Complex begin in the yard behind the Gates House. They're usually offered at 10 A.M., 11 A.M., 1 P.M., 2 P.M., and 3 P.M., but check the website or call 717/846-6452 to confirm. Public tours are curtailed when school groups descend on the historic sites.

A few blocks east of the Colonial Complex is a onetime car dealership that now houses the Heritage Trust's main offices, an extensive research library, and the **Historical Society Museum** (250 E. Market St., 10 A.M.–4 P.M. Tues.–Sat.), with more than 10,000 square feet of exhibitions on everything from quilts to tall case clocks. About half a mile east of the Colonial Complex is the **Fire Museum** (757 W. Market St., 10 A.M.–4 P.M. Sat., closed mid-Dec.–late Mar.). Its collection of firefighting artifacts includes horse-drawn fire carriages, vintage fire trucks, and old-fashioned alarm systems.

Tickets good for all Heritage Trust sites are sold at each of the sites. One-day tickets are $10 for adults and $5 for children 8–18. Two-day tickets and family passes are available.

USA Weightlifting Hall of Fame

If you've ever done bicep curls or bench presses, "York" probably rings a bell. The name is emblazoned on barbells, dumbbells, and other weightlifting equipment made by York Barbell, founded in York in 1932. The company is now Canadian-owned, but it still has administrative offices just north of the city. A statue of a weightlifter in a blue singlet, barbell hoisted overhead, still revolves atop the adjacent factory, turning the heads of motorists on nearby I-83. And the Weightlifting Hall of Fame (3300 Board Rd., York, 800/358-9675, www.yorkbarbell.com, 10 A.M.–4:30 P.M. Mon.–Sat.,

free admission) still welcomes fans of strength sports. Located on the first floor of York Barbell's administrative building, the Hall of Fame is part history museum and part homage to company founder and weightlifting legend Bob Hoffman. Raised near Pittsburgh, Hoffman was a sickly, reed-thin kid. In 1919, after serving overseas in World War I, he moved to York and cofounded an oil burner company. Determined to build not just his business but also his body, Hoffman bought a barbell. By the late 1920s, the now-buff businessman was training other lifters and hiring them to work in his factory, which he eventually transformed from York Oil Burner into York Barbell. In 1946, when the United States won its first weightlifting world championship, four of the six teammates worked for York Barbell. Hoffman coached the U.S. Olympic team from 1948 to 1964, and in 1970, the International Weightlifting Federation crowned him the "Father of World Weightlifting." By then, York also had a fanciful title: "Muscletown USA."

A 7.5-foot bronze statue of Hoffman stands outside the entrance to the Weightlifting Hall of Fame. The two-story lobby features a bronze bust of Hoffman, who died in 1985, and dumbbells and barbells from the 19th and early 20th centuries. Exhibits trace the evolution of strength sports, highlighting legendary strongmen such as Joe "The Mighty Atom" Greenstein, whose feats of strength included biting nails in half, and John Grimek, a longtime employee of York Barbell as well as a two-time Mr. America and 1948's Mr. Universe. Highlights of the collection include a seven-foot Travis dumbbell weighing more than 1,600 pounds. Its lifter and namesake, Warren Lincoln Travis, weighed just 180 ponds during his zenith in the early 1900s.

Haines Shoe House

Worth a stop if you're tootling along U.S. 30 or Route 462 (a.k.a. the Lincoln Highway) in western York County is the Haines Shoe House (197 Shoe House Rd., Hellam, 717/840-8339, www.shoehouse.us, 11 A.M.–5 P.M. Wed.–Sun. June–Aug., 11 A.M.–5 P.M. Sat.–Sun.

Sept.–Oct., by appointment Nov.–May, admission $4.50, children 4–12 $3). Built in 1948, the shoe-shaped house was an advertising gimmick by "Shoe Wizard" Mahlon Haines, whose shoe empire grew to more than 40 stores in central Pennsylvania and northern Maryland. At first, the eccentric millionaire invited elderly couples to spend an expense-free weekend in the three-bedroom, two-bath shoe house, where they had a maid, cook, and chauffeur at their disposal. In 1950 he extended the invitation to honeymooning couples from any town with a Haines shoe store. After his death in 1962, the house became an ice cream parlor. Today the roadside oddity is a museum dedicated to Haines, who staged safaris on his nearby "Wizard Ranch" and used to stop smokers on the streets of York, offering them cash if they promised to quit.

The shoe motif is ubiquitous throughout the property. You'll find it on the wooden fence that surrounds the house and in the stained glass windows. There's even a shoe-shaped doghouse. Guided tours reveal other novelties, including a curved eating booth in the kitchen, located in the heel of the shoe house. Ice cream and other snacks are sold on site, along with kitschy gifts like shoe house lamps with lighted windows.

Maize Quest Fun Park

In 1997, Hugh McPherson carved a maze into a cornfield on Maple Lawn Farms in southern York County. It proved such a hit that in 2000, the Penn State graduate added a straw bale maze, a fence maze, and a maze of living bamboo. Year after year, Maize Quest Fun Park (2885 New Park Rd., New Park, 866/935-6738, www.mazefunpark.com) unveiled new attractions. Today it boasts more than 20, including an 80-foot-long tube slide, a maze lined with misters designed for cooling livestock, and a mammoth indoor playground. Most attractions open in early June. The signature cornfield maze, which reflects a different theme each year, is revealed in August. Themes have included "Ice Age Adventure," "Space Explorers," and "The Vikings!" Maize

Quest is open Fridays, Saturdays, and Sundays through mid-November. Admission is $9.50 for adults, $7.50 for children 2–12. The indoor playground, designed for kids ages 2–10, is open Saturdays from early December to early June. Admission for kids is $7.50; there's no charge for adults. Call or check the website for hours.

ENTERTAINMENT AND EVENTS
Performing Arts

Downtown York's **Strand-Capitol Performing Arts Center** (50 N. George St., York, 717/846-1111, www.strandcapitol.org) plays host to touring musicians, dance companies, comedians, and acrobats. The **York Symphony Orchestra** (717/812-0717, www.yorksymphony.org), which has performed without interruption since the Depression, can also be seen there. "There" is actually a five-building complex that includes two historic theaters. What's now known as the Capitol Theatre opened in 1906 as a dance hall and later became a movie house. The larger, grander Strand Theatre opened in 1925 primarily for vaudeville and silent movies. Both closed in the late 1970s as suburbia sucked the life out of downtown. But a movement to reopen them quickly took shape, and the Strand and Capitol reopened their doors in 1980 and 1981, respectively. At 500 seats, the Capitol is less than half the size of the Strand, but it boasts a restored 1927 Mighty Wurlitzer. The organ is put to use before classic film showings, which sometimes involve audience participation (e.g., singing along to *The Sound of Music* or dressing like the title character in *The Big Lebowski*). Contemporary independent and foreign films are also shown at the Capitol.

Festivals and Events

Thousands of gleaming vintage cars of every description roll into York for **Street Rod Nationals East** (901/452-4030, www.nsra-usa.com, early June, admission charged), one of about a dozen annual events hosted by the National Street Rod Association. The street rods—vintage vehicles that have been modernized with features such as air conditioning and cruise control—congregate on the grounds of the York Expo Center (334 Carlisle Ave., York, 717/848-2596, www.yorkexpo.com), where auto enthusiasts can get a close look and chat up the owners. Spectators line the streets of York for a parade of the candy-colored cars.

In September the Expo Center hosts its signature event, the 10-day **York Fair** (717/848-2596, www.yorkfair.org, opens first Friday after Labor Day, admission charged). The fair dates to 1765—11 years before the nation was founded—and bills itself as America's first and oldest. It was interrupted during the Civil War, when the fairgrounds served as a hospital for wounded soldiers, and in 1918 due to a deadly influenza outbreak. But the fair hasn't taken a hiatus since, growing larger and longer with each passing decade. It even remained open in the days following the 9/11 attacks, in celebration of American culture and spirit.

SPORTS AND RECREATION
Heritage Rail Trail

The 21-mile Heritage Rail Trail (717/840-7440, www.yorkcountyparks.org) stretches from York City to the Mason-Dixon line, where it connects to Maryland's 20-mile Northern Central Railroad Trail. Hiking, bicycling, horseback riding, cross-country skiing, and snowshoeing are permitted on the 10-foot-wide path. The parking lot for the York City trailhead is on Pershing Avenue near the Colonial Courthouse. Traversing the trail is part exercise, part history lesson. About six miles south of the reconstructed courthouse is the 370-foot Howard Tunnel, the oldest continuously operational railroad tunnel in the world. The rail line adjacent to the Heritage Rail Trail was a vital link between Washington, D.C., and points north in the 19th century. As such, it was a prime target for Confederate troops during the Civil War. After the Battle of Gettysburg, President Lincoln traveled via these rails to deliver the Gettysburg Address, stretching his legs at York County's Hanover Junction station, located on Route 616 about six miles south of U.S. 30.

Restored to its 1863 appearance, the station at the midpoint of the Heritage Rail Trail is now a Civil War museum. Another historic station at Front and Franklin Streets in New Freedom, 1.5 trail miles north of the state line, is now a railroad museum. Check the York County Parks website for information on when the museums are open.

A good place to start if you're looking to rent a bicycle is Seven Valleys, a small borough just north of Hanover Junction. There you'll find **Serenity Station** (11 Church St./Rte. 214, Seven Valleys, 717/428-9575, www.serenity-station.com, 11 A.M.–8 P.M. Mon.–Thurs., 11 A.M.–9 P.M. Fri., 8 A.M.–9 P.M. Sat., 8 A.M.–8 P.M. Sun., open until 9 P.M. daily June–Aug.), a bike shop, day spa, and restaurant rolled into one. Single, tandem, and recumbent bikes can be rented by the hour or day. Child seats and trailers are available. The Heritage Rail Trail is just behind Serenity Station, which also sells bike parts and offers repair services. Call at least 48 hours in advance if you'd like a hot stone deep tissue massage, a detox wrap, or other spa service. Serenity Station's restaurant ($5–17) offers salads, sandwiches, grilled panini and wraps, and personal pizzas. The dinner menu is a touch fancier, featuring entrées like pepper-encrusted steak tenderloin and seafood tossed with rotini pasta. Breakfast is served on Saturdays and Sundays. Also adjacent to the rail trail is **Four Springs Winery** (50 Main St., Seven Valleys, 717/428-2610, www.fourspringswinerypa .com, 1–6 P.M. Fri. and Sun., 11 A.M.–6 P.M. Sat.), one of about a dozen wineries along the UnCork York Wine Trail. It's not unusual to see spandex-clad cyclists sampling the fruit-driven wines before continuing on their way.

Kayaking

Worth a visit if only to gaze at the scenic Susquehanna River from its front porch, **Shank's Mare** (2092 Long Level Rd., Wrightsville, 717/252-1616, www.shanksmare .com, 10 A.M.–8 P.M. Mon.–Fri., 10 A.M.–5 P.M. Sat., noon–5 P.M. Sun. in summer, call or check website for non-summer hours) rents

Shank's Mare outfitters

single, tandem, and triple kayaks. You don't need any experience to take to the water in one of the outfitter's sit-on-top kayaks. Birders come from hundreds of miles away to paddle to the Conejohela Flats, a series of small islands and mud flats that attract scores of migratory shorebirds in spring and fall. On a calm day, it takes about 40 minutes to paddle from Shank's Mare to the Audubon-designated Important Bird Area.

The family-owned outfitter, housed in an 1890s general store, offers guided paddles, kayaking instruction, hiking tours of Moon Dancer Vineyards and other nearby areas, and programs on topics such as local geology and kayak fishing. It also sells kayaks, cross-country skiing gear, local trail maps, and outdoor clothing, including shirts, hats, and other items emblazoned with its motto, "Go Play Outside." The 193-mile **Mason Dixon Trail** (www.masondixontrail.org) passes right by Shank's Mare.

Ski Roundtop

About midway between York and Harrisburg,

Ski Roundtop (925 Roundtop Rd., Lewisberry, 717/432-9631, www.skiroundtop.com, 8-hour lift ticket $47–56, children 6–12 $42–49, ski rental $35, snowboard rental $40, snow tubing 1-hour session $14–20) has 16 trails, three terrain parks, and one half-pipe. In addition to all-day and nighttime lift tickets, the resort offers four- and eight-hour "flex" tickets activated at the time of purchase. One- and two-hour tickets are available for snow tubing sessions, which begin at the top of each hour. Kids 2–4 have a tubing hill all to themselves and can ride all day for just $7. Homemade contraptions of cardboard, tape, and glue careen down the tubing runs during Ski Roundtop's annual **Cardboard Derby,** held January 31.

Roundtop Mountain Adventures, the resort's summertime persona, features the Vertical Trek, a descent of more than 600 vertical feet via zip lines, rope bridges, Tarzan swings, and other means. Reservations are highly recommended for the treks, which can take up to four hours. Other summertime activities include tubing on turf-covered runs, bumper boating, and "zorbing"—rolling downhill in a large inflatable orb. The resort's paintball facility is open year-round. Groups can polish their teamwork skills on a pair of ropes courses.

AvalancheXpress

The snow tubing hill at York's Heritage Hills Golf Resort, AvalancheXpress (2700 Mount Rose Ave., York, 877/782-9752, www .avalanchexpress.com, day pass $18–26, children 6 and under $10–14), has multiple runs ranging from a kiddie slope to "Xtreme" lanes with daredevils in mind. Plan to make a day of it; AvalancheXpress doesn't sell passes by the hour. There are fire pits, picnic tables, outdoor concessions, and an indoor bar for relaxing and refueling between runs. You'll find the shortest lines on weekdays and the longest on Saturday afternoons.

Spectator Sports

Almost four decades after the York White Roses hung up their uniforms, professional baseball returned to York. The **York Revolution** (Sovereign Bank Stadium, 5 Brooks Robinson Way, York, 717/801-4487, www.york revolution.com), a member of the Atlantic League of Professional Baseball, played its inaugural season in 2007. The Revs have a friendly rivalry with the Lancaster Barnstormers across the Susquehanna River, with each trying to best the other in a "War of the Roses" series. (The name is a nod to the War of the Roses between the Houses of York and Lancaster in 15th-century England.)

ACCOMMODATIONS

Built during the Roaring Twenties, **◖ The Yorktowne Hotel** (48 E. Market St., York, 717/848-1111, www.yorktowne.com, $109–300) is resplendent with high ceilings, brass and crystal chandeliers, and wood paneling. Just as impressive is the service; some of the staff have worked at the downtown landmark for upwards of 20 years. The Yorktowne is conveniently located within walking distance of the Colonial Complex, the northern terminus of the Heritage Rail Trail, Central Market, and the Strand-Capitol Performing Arts Center.

And it's home to **The Commonwealth Room** (5:30–9:30 P.M. Tues.–Sat., $26–38), York County's only AAA Four Diamond restaurant, plus a cocktail lounge open nightly until 1:30 A.M. The 121 guest rooms and suites have period furnishings and modern conveniences including complimentary Internet access.

You don't have to be a golfer to appreciate the amenities at **Heritage Hills Golf Resort** (2700 Mount Rose Ave., York, 877/782-9752, www.hhgr.com, $149–179). Just minutes from downtown York, the property boasts a spa open seven days a week, an 18-hole mini golf course, and a busy entertainment calendar. The patio of Knickers Pub, a casual eatery overlooking the golf course, is a locals' favorite in summertime. AvalancheXpress, the resort's snow tubing hill, draws crowds in winter. An indoor water park is in the works. If golf is your thing, be sure to inquire about "stay-and-play" packages. Heritage Hills also offers spa packages, snow tubing packages, romantic packages, and even hot air balloon packages. (Balloons lift off from the golf course at sunrise or before sunset.)

York County has no shortage of excellent B&Bs. Among them: the **Lady Linden Bed and Breakfast** (505 Linden Ave., York, 717/843-2929, www.ladylindenbedand breakfast.com, $129), a meticulously restored 1887 Queen Anne Victorian with two guest suites. The house is impeccably decorated, the linens are silky soft, and breakfast is a four-course affair. **The Beechmont** (315 Broadway, Hanover, 800/553-7009, $109–169) is an excellent choice in southern York County. Owner Kathryn White received the Pennsylvania Tourism & Lodging Association's Innkeeper of the Year Award in 2009. The Select Registry inn with its seven guest accommodations is convenient to historic Gettysburg. Now an oasis of calm, the house witnessed the Battle of Hanover, which delayed a Confederate cavalry's arrival at the more famous Battle of Gettysburg. White is a font of information about Hanover's role in the Civil War—and a whiz in the kitchen. Exquisite breakfasts are served by candlelight; homemade cookies or other treats are offered in the evenings. A two-night minimum stay applies on weekends April–November.

FOOD

Across the street from York's Central Market, the **White Rose Bar & Grill** (48 N. Beaver St., York, 717/848-5369, www.whiterosebar andgrill.com, kitchen 11 A.M.–10 P.M. Sun.–Thurs. and 11 A.M.–11 P.M. Fri.–Sat., bar open until 2 A.M. Mon.–Sat. and midnight Sun., $5–35) dates to the 1930s. Extensive renovations in recent years have given it a thoroughly modern feel. The appetizer menu includes oysters on the half shell, seared sushi-grade tuna, and plenty of deep-fried goodies, but nothing compares to the soft pretzel sticks topped with crab dip and melted cheese. Meal options range from a simple BLT to Hereford beef filet mignon. Order from the Hot Rock Menu and your seafood or steak will arrive at the table on a hot volcanic rock, where it'll continue to cook while you dig in.

If raw is how you like it, try **Keo Asian Grill and Sushi Restaurant** (15 S. George St., York, 717/848-2510, www.keoasian.com, 11 A.M.–4 P.M. Mon.–Wed., 11 A.M.–9 P.M. Thurs.–Sat., $6–14), a relative newcomer to downtown York's dining scene. The space is small, which can mean a wait during the lunchtime rush, but the sushi is consistently good. Don't eat sushi? Keo has an extensive menu of beef, chicken, seafood, and vegetarian dishes that reflect the cooking traditions of China, Thailand, and other far reaches.

Fresh, seasonal American cuisine is the focus at **Blue Moon** (361 W. Market St., York, 717/854-6664, www.bluemoonfresh.com, lunch 11:30 A.M.–2:30 P.M. Tues.–Fri., dinner 4:30–9:30 P.M. Mon.–Sat., lunch $10–15, dinner $18–36), a lovely bistro with white tablecloths, walls decked with original art, and nary a hint of pretension. The happy hour—Thursdays from 5:30–7:30 P.M.—is among the best around, complete with complimentary hors d'oeuvres. Take your martini to the backyard deck if the weather's nice.

York's most impressive martini list can be found at ◖ **The Left Bank** (120 N. George St., York, 717/843-8010, www.leftbankyork .com, lunch 11 A.M. Tues.–Fri., dinner 4 P.M. Mon.–Sat., $10–34), a chef-owned fine dining restaurant with a big-city feel. This is where Yorkers come on special occasions. Don't think "Philly cheesesteak" and "fancy" belong in the same sentence? You haven't tried chef David Albright's cheesesteak appetizer, made with beef tenderloin, bruschetta, and basil aioli. The seafood entrées are outstanding, as is the service. Don't hesitate to ask the waitstaff for wine recommendations.

If your visit to York County includes wine-tasting at Moon Dancer Vineyards or kayaking from Shank's Mare, plan on dining at the **John Wright Restaurant** (N. Front St., Wrightsville, 717/252-0416, www.johnwright restaurant.com, 8 A.M.–3 P.M. Mon.–Wed., 8 A.M.–9 P.M. Thurs.–Sat., 11 A.M.–4 P.M. Sun., $4–20), which occupies a restored warehouse along the Susquehanna River. Heck, plan on dining there if you're anywhere within a 20-mile radius. The casual atmosphere, comfort foods, and killer views make it worth a drive. (You can also kayak to it.) Come for Sunday brunch if you get the chance, when the menu includes French toast with roasted peaches, smoked salmon soufflé, and a 5-ounce burger with your choice of fixings, plus $3 Bloody Marys and mimosas. Also on premises: the John Wright Store (8 A.M.–5 P.M. Mon.–Wed., 8 A.M.–8 P.M. Thurs.–Sat., 11 A.M.–5 P.M. Sun.), which sells cast iron home and garden products made by the locally based company of the same name as well as accessories by the likes of Vera Bradley.

INFORMATION

If you're arriving in York County via I-83 north, look for the state-run welcome center 2.5 miles north of the Pennsylvania-Maryland line. Personalized travel counseling is available 7 A.M.–7 P.M. daily; the restrooms are always open.

Visit the website of the **York County Convention & Visitors Bureau** (717/852-9675, www.yorkpa.org) to request a free visitors guide or peruse a digital version. The CVB operates a visitors center in downtown York (155 W. Market St., 9:30 A.M.–4 P.M. daily) and another at the Harley-Davidson plant (1425 Eden Rd., York, 9 A.M.–5 P.M. daily). For information about Pennsylvania Dutch Country as a whole, visit www.dutch countryroads.com.

GETTING THERE AND AROUND

York County shares its southern border with Maryland. Its county seat and largest municipality, York, is about 50 miles north of Baltimore and 25 miles south of Harrisburg via I-83. U.S. 30 provides east–west access to the city, which is about 30 miles from Gettysburg to its west and Lancaster to its east.

Harrisburg International Airport (888/235-9442, www.flyhia.com), about half an hour's drive from York, is served by Air Canada, AirTran Airways, Continental Airlines, Delta Air Lines, United Airlines, and US Airways. They offer daily nonstop service to about a dozen destinations. Note that while locals refer to the airport as HIA, its Federal Aviation Administration booking code is MDT. That's because of its physical location in the borough of Middletown, about eight miles south of Harrisburg. **Baltimore/Washington International Thurgood Marshall Airport** (800/435-9294, www.bwiairport.com) is farther—about an hour from York assuming minimal traffic—but considerably larger. It's served by about 25 commercial airlines.

Intercity bus service to York is available through **Greyhound** (800/231-2222, www.greyhound.com) and its interline partners. York County's public bus system is **Rabbittransit** (800/632-9063, www.rabbittransit.org).

Gettysburg and Vicinity

Few places in America have the name recognition of Gettysburg. There's hardly an eighth grader who hasn't heard of the town, which has but 8,000 residents and welcomes some three million visitors a year. It earned its place in the history books in 1863, when it was the setting for the Civil War's bloodiest battle and President Abraham Lincoln's most famous speech. The former took place in July of that year, when more than 165,000 soldiers converged on the crossroads town. Over the first three days of the month, a Union army under the command of General George G. Meade desperately and successfully defended its home territory from General Robert E. Lee's Confederate forces. The war would continue for almost two more years, but the Confederacy's hopes for independence effectively died on the Gettysburg battlefield. The hellish battle's human toll was astronomical: 51,000 soldiers were dead, wounded, or missing. Interestingly, only one of Gettysburg's 2,400 citizens was killed during the biggest battle ever fought on this continent. The casualty was a young woman named Jennie Wade, and the bullet-riddled house in which she died is now a museum named for her.

In the aftermath of the battle, the townspeople dedicated themselves to caring for the wounded and burying the dead. A group of prominent residents convinced the state to help fund the purchase of a portion of the battlefield to serve as a final resting place for the Union's defenders. Gettysburg attorney David Wills was appointed to coordinate the establishment of the Soldiers' National Cemetery, and he invited President Lincoln to deliver "a few appropriate remarks" at the dedication ceremony on November 19. The lanky commander-in-chief arrived by train the previous day and strolled down Carlisle Street to Wills's stately home on the town square. There, in a second-floor bedroom, he polished his talk. The National Park Service acquired the house in 2004 and opened it as a museum in 2009. Lincoln was not the featured speaker at the

The Pennsylvania memorial, Gettysburg's most visited, is a tribute to all the Pennsylvania soldiers who fought there.

These simple stones in Gettysburg National Cemetery mark the graves of unidentified soldiers who were killed in the battles.

dedication of the cemetery. That honor went to politician and orator Edward Everett, who waxed on for two hours. But Lincoln's two-minute Gettysburg Address—so succinct that a photographer on the scene failed to snap a picture—is regarded as the rhetorical zenith of his career and one of the greatest speeches in history.

America's four-year civil war was fought on many battlegrounds, but none is as hallowed as Gettysburg's. Established in 1895, Gettysburg National Military Park was the first historic site owned by the U.S. government. As the only major Civil War battlefield in a northern state and an easy trip from population centers such as Philadelphia and Baltimore, it attracted scores of veterans and other visitors. The battlefield's popularity as a tourist destination bred commercial development in the 20th century. At one point there was even a casino on what is now park property. In recent years, preservationists have gotten the upper hand. Commercial establishments have been given

the boot. Billboards have vanished. In 2000, on the anniversary of the final day of the battle, locals cheered as an observation tower built in the 1970s on private land adjacent to the park was demolished with explosives. The National Park Service is even removing trees from parts of the battlefield, planting them in others, and reconstructing long-gone farm lanes and roads so that the landscape looks more like it did in 1863. Bottom line: There hasn't been a better time to visit Gettysburg in the last century. The picture of what transpired there is getting clearer and clearer.

When to visit? That depends on your interests and tolerance for crowds. The Gettysburg area is busiest in early July, during the annual battle reenactment, which is held not on the battlefield but on private land. The town swarms with tourists and rifle-toting reenactors, and the weather tends toward hot and humid. Visitation tapers off as the summer draws to a close, then picks up in October, when paranormal enthusiasts flock to what they believe is one of the most haunted places in the country. Mid-November brings scores of Lincoln scholars and admirers. They discuss his life and legacy at an annual symposium before joining in a town-wide celebration of his famous address. Winter is the slow season, an ideal time for hushed contemplation of the carnage that took place here and the courage that shaped this country. Some Gettysburg attractions are closed during the coldest months, but the battlefield is open daily year-round. Things pick up in April with the arrival of busload after busload of schoolchildren. By June, tourism is in full swing.

The battlefield is certainly the area's biggest draw, but there are more than a dozen other sights of interest to history buffs. Downtown Gettysburg is itself a historical attraction: About 60 percent of its buildings predate the battle. One of the most popular tourist stops isn't about history at all. It's a museum housing one man's collection of elephants (man-made, not living). Another non-historical attraction, the Land of Little Horses (living, not man-made), scores big with kids.

GETTYSBURG NATIONAL MILITARY PARK

Expect to spend the better part of a day at Gettysburg National Military Park (717/334-1124, ext. 8023, www.nps.gov/gett, 6 A.M.–10 P.M. daily Apr.–Oct., 6 A.M.–7 P.M. daily Nov.–Mar., free admission), site of the Civil War's biggest and bloodiest battle. Run by the National Park Service, the 6,000-acre battlefield is not only one of the nation's most popular historical attractions but also one of the world's most extraordinary sculpture gardens. It's dotted with more than 1,300 monuments, markers, and memorials. The oldest was dedicated on July 1, 1869, the sixth anniversary of the first day of fighting. State after state commissioned monuments in the late 1800s. Visitors encounter equestrian bronzes of the battle's commanders, tributes to common soldiers, a statue of a civilian hero, and another of a priest who gave absolution to Irish soldiers as they prepared for battle.

It's best to begin your visit at the **Museum and Visitor Center** (1195 Baltimore Pike/Rte. 97, Gettysburg, 717/338-1243, reservations

the Louisiana monument, sculpted by Donald De Lue

the North Carolina monument, sculpted by Gutzon Borglum

© CARL SHUMAN

The cyclorama in the Visitor Center is a 360-degree painting of Pickett's Charge.

717/334-2436, www.gettysburgfoundation.org, 8 A.M.–6 P.M. daily Apr.–Oct., 8 A.M.–5 P.M. daily Nov.–Mar., admission to film/cyclorama/museum $10.50, seniors $9.50, children 6–18 $6.50), operated by the nonprofit Gettysburg Foundation. There you can orient yourself to the park and learn about the nightmarish clash of armies. Be sure to ask for a schedule of lectures, guided walks, and other special programs, which are especially frequent from mid-June through mid-August. If you plan on touring the battlefield on your own, pick up an official park map and guide (also available at www.nps.gov/gett). It offers a 24-mile auto tour with 16 stops on the battlefield and a couple more in downtown Gettysburg. Brief descriptions of what transpired at each battlefield stop are included. For detailed descriptions of the three-day battle, you can buy an audio tour CD in the museum bookstore or hire a federally licensed guide, who for $55 will get behind the wheel of your car and take you and as many as five other passengers on a two-hour personalized tour. The highly knowledgeable guides

are available on a first-come, first-served basis as soon as the Visitor Center opens, but reservations are recommended. Bus tours with a licensed guide ($28 per person, children 6–12 $17) are also offered.

The Visitor Center, which opened in 2008, is home to a colossal cyclorama depicting Pickett's Charge, a futile infantry assault ordered by Confederate General Robert E. Lee on the final day of battle. It's said that veterans wept at the sight of artist Paul Philippoteaux's 360-degree painting when it was unveiled in 1884. In the 1960s the Park Service commissioned architect Richard Neutra to create a cylindrical home for the masterpiece. But climate control proved a problem in Neutra's modernistic building, and the cyclorama was rehung in the new Visitor Center after several years of painstaking and costly restoration. The largest painting in the country—42 feet high and slightly longer than a football field—is now displayed with a canopy overhead and a diorama that carries the moving scene into the foreground, features that had been lost for more than a century. A sound and light show amps up the drama. The cyclorama experience is preceded by a 22-minute film, *A New Birth of Freedom,* narrated by Morgan Freeman. Timed tickets are issued for the film and cyclorama. Ticket holders can explore the **Gettysburg Museum of the American Civil War** at their own pace. Its 12 galleries include artifacts, films, and interactive exhibits that place the Battle of Gettysburg in the larger context of the deadliest war in American history.

The **Gettysburg National Cemetery,** where President Lincoln delivered his famous Gettysburg Address, is a short walk from the Visitor Center. It's open from dawn to sunset and closed to vehicular traffic. Walking tour brochures are available at the Visitor Center and can be downloaded from the Park Service's Gettysburg website. Work on the cemetery, located on the battlefield, began soon after the bloodshed ended. Thousands of Union and Confederate dead had been hastily buried on or near the battlefield, many of them in shallow graves. Heavy rains would expose decaying bodies, a grisly sight that helped convince Pennsylvania governor Andrew Curtin to appropriate state funds for the cemetery project. About 3,500 Union soldiers were interred there. The Confederate dead remained in scattered graves until the 1870s, when they were relocated to cemeteries in the south. Today the Soldiers' National Cemetery is the final resting place for veterans from all of America's wars through Vietnam. It's the setting for several annual events, including a Memorial Day service and a commemoration of the Gettysburg Address held each November.

Adjacent to the battlefield is the **Eisenhower National Historic Site** (717/338-9114, ext. 10, www.nps.gov/eise, 9 A.M.–4 P.M. daily, admission $7.50, children 6–12 $5), the one-time home and farm of President Dwight D. Eisenhower. The Texas-born Army general and 34th president first visited Gettysburg as a cadet at the U.S. Military Academy at West Point and returned during World War I to run a training camp. After commanding the Allied forces during the second World War, "Ike"

came to Gettysburg with his wife, Mamie, in search of a retirement home. They bought a 189-acre farm in 1950, but retirement eluded them. General Eisenhower left for Europe to assume command of the North Atlantic Treaty Organization, returning to the United States to run for president in 1952. During his two-term presidency, the Eisenhowers spent weekends and holidays at their Gettysburg home. The president entertained world leaders there, introducing them to his show herd of black Angus cattle and chatting with them on his porch. The Eisenhowers finally retired to their farm in 1961 and donated it to the National Park Service in 1967, two years before the general's death. Mrs. Eisenhower continued to live there until her death in 1979. The house has changed little since then. Furnishings include a coffee table given to the Eisenhowers by the first lady of South Korea, a rug from the shah of Iran, and a desk fashioned from old floorboards removed from the White House during a 1948 renovation. Visitors can also explore the grounds, which include a putting green, a skeet range, rose gardens, and a garage that still houses the Eisenhowers' jeep, golf carts, and station wagon. Some 40 to 50 Angus still graze the pastures. Due to limited on-site parking and space in the home, visitors must arrive by shuttle bus from the Visitor Center at Gettysburg National Military Park.

OTHER SIGHTS
David Wills House
In the aftermath of the Battle of Gettysburg, when dead and wounded soldiers outnumbered civilians 11 to one, the home of local attorney David Wills became a center of recovery efforts. He gathered supplies for the wounded, sought compensation for farmers who'd suffered losses during the battle, and coordinated the establishment of a permanent cemetery for the Union dead. Less than three weeks before the dedication of the cemetery, Wills wrote a letter to President Abraham Lincoln inviting him to deliver "a few appropriate remarks" at the event. He had already booking famed orator Edward Everett as the main speaker. The

President Lincoln points to the bedroom in the David Wills House where he slept the night before he delivered the Gettysburg Address in a statue titled *Return Visit*.

president accepted and arrived in Gettysburg a day ahead of the November 19 dedication. Mrs. Wills had prepared her own bedroom for the president. It was there that he put the finishing touches on his Gettysburg Address. Admirers gathered outside the house could see him pacing back and forth through the second-story windows.

In 2009, on Lincoln's 200th birthday, the National Park Service opened the house as a museum that tells the story of the town's recovery and Lincoln's visit. The David Wills House (8 Lincoln Square, Gettysburg, 866/486-5735, www.davidwillshouse.org, 9 A.M.–6 P.M. daily May–Aug., 9 A.M.–5 P.M. daily except Tues. Mar.–Apr. and Sept.–Nov., 9 A.M.–5 P.M. daily except Tues. and Wed. Dec.–Feb., admission $6.50, seniors $5.50, children 6–18 $4) features the recreated Lincoln bedroom with Mrs. Wills's original bed. The office where David Wills received letters from families looking for sons lost in battle is also restored to its 1863 appearance. Other rooms have exhibits on Gettysburg before and after the battle,

Lincoln's immortal words, and the preservation and restoration of the Wills house. The collection includes Lincoln's saddle cover and a telegram sent to the president at the house.

There's a municipal parking garage a block away on Race Horse Alley. Freedom Transit (717/846-7433, www.ridethetrolley.com) trolleys provide service from the Gettysburg National Military Park Museum and Visitor Center and other locations.

Shriver and Jennie Wade Houses

Just a few blocks from the David Wills House are two house museums that explore the civilian experience during the Civil War. Tours of the **Shriver House Museum** (309 Baltimore St., Gettysburg, 717/337-2800, www.shriverhouse .org, 10 A.M.–5 P.M. Mon.–Sat. and noon–5 P.M. Sun. Apr.–mid-Nov., 10 A.M.–5 P.M. Sat. in Dec., 10 A.M.–5 P.M. Sat. and 10 A.M.–2 P.M. Sun. in Mar., admission $7.50, seniors $6.85, children under 13 $4.85) are conducted by guides in period attire. Candlelight tours are offered on Saturday evenings in December,

GETTYSBURG GUIDES

It's easy to explore Gettysburg on your own and especially so when you have this book in hand. But if you're hazy on Civil War history, a tour can make for a richer experience. Tour operators are a dime a dozen. Which one is right for you depends on your preferred mode of transport and whether you're keen on a live guide or satisfied with recorded commentary.

Many Gettysburg tours are led by members of the **Association of Licensed Battlefield Guides** (717/337-1709, www.gettysburgtourguides.org). These guys have spent years if not decades studying the Battle of Gettysburg. Licensure applicants must first pass a written exam given every other year. The highest scorers must prove themselves further by passing an oral test. If you're the sort who appreciates a lot of detail and asks a lot of questions, hire a licensed guide who will take the wheel of your car and show you around. A standard auto tour of the battlefield is two hours long. Guides are available on a first-come, first-served basis at the Gettysburg National Military Park Museum and Visitor Center (1195 Baltimore Pike/Rte. 97, Gettysburg, 8 A.M.-6 P.M. daily Apr.-Oct., 8 A.M.-5 P.M. daily Nov.-Mar.). You can also reserve a tour in advance by calling 717/334-2436 or visiting www.gettysburgfoundation.org. During busy times of year, it's not unusual for all available guides to be booked up early in the day. Guide fees are $55 for a vehicle of 1-6 people, $70 for a vehicle of 7-15. It's customary to tip your guide if you're satisfied. Bus tours with a licensed guide ($28 per person, children 6-12 $17) also leave from the visitors center. Allow 2.5 hours for the bus tour. If you'd like a specialized tour of the battlefield or town, contact the Association of Licensed Battlefield Guides directly.

Bus tours with a licensed guide also depart from the **Gettysburg Tour Center** (778 Baltimore St., Gettysburg, 717/334-6296, www.gettysburgbattlefieldtours.com), located across from the Soldiers' National Cemetery. But the commercial tour company is best known for its open-air double-decker bus tours, featuring "dramatized audio" complete with booming cannons and cracking rifles. The two-hour tour ($24.95 per person, children 6-12 $14) is offered so long as weather permits. Gettysburg Tour Center operates several area attractions, including the Jennie Wade House and the Hall of Presidents and First Ladies. Combo packages are available.

You can feel like General Lee by touring the battlefield on horseback. **Artillery Ridge Campground** (610 Taneytown Rd., Gettysburg, 717/334-1288, www.artilleryridge.com), just across the street from the battlefield, offers two-hour horseback tours ($72 per person) daily April through October and weekends in November. When a licensed guide can't be along for the tour, riders listen to a recorded narrative. Riding experience isn't necessary; reservations are. Another option: gliding around the battlefield on a Segway. **Seg-Tours** (717/253-7987, www.segtours.com) offers a 2.5-hour tour that takes in the most famous battlefield sites ($65 per person) and a shorter tour to a lesser-known part of the battlefield ($45 per person). Riders listen to a recorded narrative as they're escorted along a prescribed route. For an additional fee, a licensed guide will come along for the ride. Reservations are recommended for audio tours and required if you want a live guide. The SegTours field office is in the rear parking lot of the Reliance Mine Saloon on Taneytown Road (Route 134), about 100 yards north of the entrance to the Soldiers' National Cemetery. Tours depart on a regular schedule March-November.

If you want to burn off some calories while exploring the battlefield, take a bicycle tour. **GettysBike** (241 Steinwehr Ave., Gettysburg, 717/752-7752, www.gettysbike.com) tours generally last three hours and cover nine miles. A licensed guide always comes along. Group tours are $61 per person, $30 for children 13 and under. Bring your own bike for a discount. Families with children under 10

© ANNA DUBROVSKY

Licensed Battlefield Guide Terry Latschar leads a horseback tour of the battlefield.

must reserve a private tour, which costs $102 per person, $52 per child. Reservations are required.

While most tours focus on the battlefield and the clashes of troops that culminated in a Union victory, the nonprofit **Main Street Gettysburg** (717/339-6161, www.mainstreet-gettysburg.org) offers guided walking tours of downtown that illumine the civilian experience. One need only to look at a map of Gettysburg National Military Park to realize that the town must have been deeply scarred. The battlefield enfolds the town – the last in America to be occupied by an invading army. When the bullets stopped flying, Gettysburg citizens emerged from hiding places to an Armageddon-like scene. The town became a hospital and morgue and every citizen a first responder. Offered April through October, the 90-minute walking tours ($10 per person, seniors and children 5-12 $8) depart

from the historic Gettysburg Hotel at 1 Lincoln Square.

Gettysburg's "nearly departed" are the subject of much interest within the paranormal community. The site of so much Civil War carnage is regarded as one of the most haunted places in the county. If you're not terribly squeamish, an evening ghost-themed tour may be for you. The original and most reputable operator is **Ghosts of Gettysburg** (271 Baltimore St., Gettysburg, 717/337-0445, www.ghostsofgettysburg.com), open every season but winter. Its walking and bus tours, led by guides in period attire with candle lanterns in hand, are based on the books of historian, ghost hunter, and former National Park Service ranger Mark Nesbitt. Walking tours are $9.50-10 per person, free for children 7 and under. Bus tours are $18 per person, $16 for children 5-10, and off-limits to children under 5.

when the house is decorated for Christmas, 1860s style. George Washington Shriver paid $290 in 1860 for what was then considered a double lot on the edge of town. He built a home for his family, opening a saloon in the cellar and a 10-pin bowling alley in an adjacent building. The family was just settling in when the Civil War erupted in 1861 and Shriver answered President Lincoln's call for troops. When the war came to Gettysburg in the summer of 1863, he was still away. While his wife, Hettie, and two young daughters hunkered down at her parents' farm about three miles away, Confederate soldiers occupied their home. Today visitors learn about life during the Civil War as they tour all four floors of the house, including the attic used by Confederate sharpshooters. The bowling alley is no longer standing, but the saloon has been recreated. During the 1996 restoration of the Shriver home, three live Civil War bullets and period medical supplies were discovered under floorboards. They're among the artifacts displayed in the museum shop next door.

The nearby **Jennie Wade House** (548 Baltimore St., Gettysburg, 717/334-4100, www .gettysburgbattlefieldtours.com, 9 A.M.–7 P.M. daily in summer, 9 A.M.–5 P.M. in spring and fall, admission $7.25, children 6–12 $3.50) is a shrine to its namesake, the only civilian casualty of the Battle of Gettysburg. Jennie Wade was baking bread for Union soldiers when bullets ripped through the door of the house, taking her life. She was 20 years old and engaged to a childhood friend who'd been mustered into the service two years earlier. He died just nine days later of wounds sustained in a Virginia battle, never knowing his sweetheart's fate.

General Lee's Headquarters Museum

On the first day of the Battle of Gettysburg, Confederate General Robert E. Lee established his personal headquarters in a stone house at the center and rear of his battle lines. There, he and his commanders pondered the problems of the great battle, which ended in a victory for the Union. Fifty-nine years after Lee escaped south, the house was opened to the public as a museum named for him. General Lee's Headquarters Museum (401 Buford Ave., Gettysburg, 717/334-3141, www.civilwarhead quarters.com, 9 A.M.–5 P.M. mid-Mar.–Nov., extended summer hours, admission $3, free for children under 16 and local residents) is one of the oldest museums in Gettysburg and unique in its focus on the Confederate cause. It's also unique in that visitors can spend a night upstairs. Call 717/334-3141 or visit www .thegettysburgaddress.com for more information about the **Quality Inn at General Lee's Headquarters** ($75–240). The historic inn has hosted such bigwigs as General George Patton and President Dwight Eisenhower as well as the last surviving Confederate widow.

Wax Museums

The little town of Gettysburg is home to not one but two wax museums. More than 300 life-sized wax figures depict events of the nation's deadliest war at the **American Civil War Museum** (297 Steinwehr Ave., Gettysburg, 717/334-6245, www.gettysburgmuseum.com, 9 A.M.–5 P.M. daily Mar.–Dec., open weekends and holidays in Jan. and Feb., extended spring and summer hours, admission $5.50, children 6–17 $3). Visitors learn about the economical, social, and political causes of the war, the assassination of President Abraham Lincoln, and everything in between. The sounds of bullets and battle cries echo in the auditorium, where the Battle of Gettysburg is recreated. The on-site **Gettysburg Gift Center,** 3,200 square feet of collectibles, art, books, games, clothing, and home decor, is arguably the best gift shop in town.

A stone's throw from the main entrance to Soldiers' National Cemetery, the **Hall of Presidents and First Ladies** (789 Baltimore St., Gettysburg, 717/334-5717, www.gettys burgbattlefieldtours.com, 9 A.M.–7 P.M. in summer, 9 A.M.–5 P.M. in spring and fall, admission $7.25, children 6–12 $3.50) features wax figures of every American president. Extra attention is paid to 34th President Dwight D. Eisenhower, who bought a home in Gettysburg not long before winning the presidency and lived out his days there. The museum also has a collection of doll-sized first ladies in their inaugural gowns.

Land of Little Horses Farm Park

Admission isn't cheap, but the Land of Little Horses (125 Glenwood Dr., Gettysburg, 717/334-7259, Dec.–Mar. 717/334-5236, www.landoflittlehorses.com, 10 A.M.–5 P.M. Mon.–Sat. early June–late Aug., Sat. and Sun. only through Oct., admission $13.95, children 2–11 $11.95) is a hit with little 'uns. Just a few miles west of downtown Gettysburg, the "performing animal theme park" is home to not only miniature horses but also goats, sheep, donkeys, emus, and other critters happy to eat out of your hand. The performers among them take the stage twice daily Monday through Saturday and once on Sunday. Two dollars buys a wagon or pony ride. (Alas, if you're over 70 pounds, no pony ride for you.) A gift shop, snack bar, and guesthouse are on-site.

Mister Ed's Elephant Museum

Ed Gotwalt's passion for all things pachyderm started on his wedding day more than 40 years ago, when he received an elephant knickknack as a good luck charm. By 1975 his elephant collection had grown so large that his wife made him open a museum to get them out of the house. Miss Ellie Phant, a life-sized talking elephant with animated eyes and ears, greets visitors at Mister Ed's Elephant Museum (6019 Chambersburg Rd., Orrtanna, 717/352-3792, www.mistereds.com, 10 A.M.–5 P.M. daily, free admission), located on U.S. 30 about 12 miles west of Gettysburg. It doesn't cost a cent to see Gotwalt's collection, which ballooned to more than 10,000 elephants after an anonymous donor left him some 4,000 in her will. There are stone elephants, wood elephants, metal elephants, and plush elephants. There's an elephant potty chair and an elephant hair dryer. There are even elephant-embroidered pillowcases that once belonged to Cher. It's safe to say you'll never see any place like it. Elephants aren't the only draw. A onetime peanut dealer,

Gotwalt sells mountains of nuts and candy, including nostalgic varieties like wax bottles and Pez.

Appalachian Trail Museum

After 12 years in the making, the Appalachian Trail Museum (1120 Pine Grove Rd., Gardners, 717/486-8126, www.atmuseum .org, noon–4 P.M. daily Memorial Day–Labor Day and weekends in spring and fall, free admission) opened in 2010 in a former gristmill about 20 miles north of Gettysburg. It pays tribute to pioneer hikers such as Earl Shaffer, the first person to thru-hike the trail, and "Grandma" Gatewood, so nicknamed because she was 67 when she became the first female to complete the journey alone. A pillowcase she used as a pack is among the artifacts displayed in the first museum dedicated to the famed footpath. There's even an exhibit on Ziggy, who in 1990 became the first feline to conquer the Georgia-to-Maine trail. (To be fair, the cat spent most of the journey riding on the backpack of hiker Jim "the Geek" Adams, but he contributed much in the way of mice patrol at trail shelters.) Highlights of the collection include a trail shelter that Shaffer, a native of nearby York County, built about a decade after his 1948 history-making hike. The shelter was painstakingly dismantled at its original site on a mountain north of Harrisburg and reassembled in the museum.

Visitors stand a good chance of rubbing shoulders with modern-day thru-hikers because the museum is just a few hundred yards off the A.T. in **Pine Grove Furnace State Park** (717/486-7174, www.dcnr.state.pa.us/ stateparks/parks/PineGroveFurnace.aspx), which marks the midpoint of the 2,179-mile trail. Tradition dictates that thru-hikers stop at the park's general store, across the road from the museum, and face a test of mettle known as the "half-gallon challenge." Those who succeed, i.e., eat a half gallon of ice cream, are rewarded with a commemorative wooden spoon. Word has it that chunky flavors are harder to finish.

The state park is named for an ironworks founded in 1764, and the charcoal iron furnace that operated until 1895 is still standing. A mansion built in 1829 for the ironmaster's family is now a youth hostel (717/486-7575) along the Appalachian Trail. It closed for extensive renovations in 2010 and was expected to reopen in spring 2011. The 696-acre park also features a campground and two small lakes with beaches and a boat rental. Pine Grove allows overnight parking for anyone who wants to hit the A.T., but registration at the park office is required. The office is at the intersection of Route 233 and Pine Grove Road, a few hundred feet from the museum.

National Apple Museum

Adams County, of which Gettysburg is the county seat, is one of the largest apple producers in the country and the heart of Pennsylvania's fruit belt. It's home to grower-owned applesauce maker Musselman's, a Mott's plant, and the National Apple Museum (154 W. Hanover St., Biglerville, 717/677-4556, www.national applemuseum.com, 10 A.M.–4 P.M. Sat. and 1–4 P.M. Sun. May–Oct., admission $2, seniors $1.75, children 6–16 $1). Miles and miles of orchards make for scenic drives, especially when the trees are in bloom. (See www .gettysburgwineandfruittrail.com for suggested routes north and west of Gettysburg.)

ENTERTAINMENT AND EVENTS
Performing Arts

The **Majestic Theater** (35 Carlisle St., Gettysburg, 717/337-8200, www.gettysburg majestic.org) was the largest vaudeville and silent movie theater in south-central Pennsylvania when it opened in 1925. President Dwight D. Eisenhower and First Lady Mamie Eisenhower attended performances in the 1950s, often with world leaders in tow. In 1993 the Majestic hosted the world premiere of *Gettysburg,* one of the longest films ever released by a Hollywood studio at more than four hours. Today it hosts live performances by the likes of the Moscow Circus, the Temptations, and pianist Jim Brickman. Two cinemas with stadium seating and a pair of "cuddle up" seats in every row

were added as part of a $16 million renovation in recent years. Art films are shown nightly.

Festivals and Events

The blooming of Adams County's fragrant blossoms is cause for a celebration: the **Apple Blossom Festival** (717/677-7444, www.uasd .k12.pa.us/upperadams/Fruitgrowers/festival, admission $5, children under 12 free), takes place the first weekend in May. Free orchard tours, pony and wagon rides, apple-bobbing and pie-eating contests, antique cars, arts and crafts, live entertainment, and an apple queen contest are all part of the fun. The fall harvest is occasion for Adams County's biggest to-do, the **National Apple Harvest Festival** (717/677-9413, www.appleharvest.com, first two weekends in Oct., admission $9, seniors $8, children under 12 free). Both festivals are held at the South Mountain Fair Grounds, 10 miles northwest of Gettysburg on Route 234.

A different crop gets the limelight in June.

A bin of apples sits ready for cooking at the National Apple Harvest Festival.

© GETTYSBURG CONVENTION & VISITORS BUREAU

The **Pennsylvania Lavender Festival** (145 Tract Rd., Fairfield, 717/642-6387, www .palavenderfestival.com, Father's Day weekend) is held at Willow Pond Farm in Fairfield, about 15 minutes west of Gettysburg. Owners Tom and Madeline Wajda grow more than 100 different lavenders along with other herbs and perennial plants. Festival-goers can tour the lavender field, cut their own lavender, and make lavender wands. Lectures and workshops on growing lavender, herbal medicines, cooking with fresh herbs, edible topiaries, and other topics are offered throughout the three-day festival. The certified organic farm is also open to visitors 9 A.M.–5 P.M. Thursday–Saturday from April to Christmas and noon–5 P.M. on Sundays from April to mid-June and in November and December. Visit the farm's website, www.willowpondherbs.com, for more information on its demonstration gardens and shop, which sells herbal jellies, vinegars, honeys, teas, and more.

A tradition since 1979, the **Gettysburg Bluegrass Festival** (3340 Fairfield Rd., Gettysburg, 717/642-8749, www.gettysburg bluegrass.com) is actually two four-day festivals: one in May and another in August. Both are held at Granite Hill Camping Resort, about five miles west of Gettysburg on Route 116. Top bluegrass and traditional country musicians turn out for the acclaimed festivals. Legendary mandolinist John Duffey played every one from 1979 until his death in 1996, and singer/fiddler Alison Krauss, who first played the festival as a high school senior, continued showing up through the year she was crowned Female Vocalist of the Year by the Country Music Association. Single- and multi-day tickets can be purchased at the gate (cash only) or in advance at a discount.

Thousands of reenactors take part in the annual **Gettysburg Civil War Battle Reenactment** (717/338-1525, www.gettys burgreenactment.com, early July), firing period

© GETTYSBURG CONVENTION & VISITORS BUREAU

Union soldiers fire a cannon during the annual Gettysburg Civil War Battle Reenactment.

Confederate soldiers line up in formation before reenacting a battle during the annual event.

weapons and feigning death on farm fields just a few miles from the original battlefield. Half a dozen clashes are staged over several days. Spectators can stroll through the soldiers' camps, listen to live Civil War music and period speakers, watch period demonstrations, and shop for period wares. Admission at the gate is $30 for adults, $15 for children 6–12. You'll save if you order tickets in advance. Arrive early to claim a spot near the front of battle viewing areas. It's a good idea to bring folding chairs, binoculars, and sunscreen. Limited bleacher seating is available for an additional $10 per person per day and usually sells out before the event.

A host of events commemorate President Abraham Lincoln's most famous speech, delivered at the dedication of the Soldiers' National Cemetery less than five months after the Battle of Gettysburg. Held on the anniversary of his Gettysburg Address, **Dedication Day** (717/334-1124, www.nps.gov/gett, Nov. 19) begins with a wreath-laying ceremony at the cemetery. Locally based and nationally renowned Lincoln actor Jim Getty recites the short address after an oration by a person of note. Past speakers have included actor Richard Dreyfuss, newsman Tom Brokaw, aviator Neil Armstrong, and Chief Justice William Rehnquist. The Saturday closest to November 19 is **Remembrance Day** (717/334-6274, www.gettysburg.travel) in Gettysburg. A parade of reenactors—Union and Confederate troops, drummer boys and generals on horseback, women and children in 1800s attire—winds through town and ends at the national military park. As the day draws to a close, a luminary candle is placed on each Civil War grave in the national cemetery. The cost to sponsor a candle for the **Remembrance Illumination** (717/338-1243, www.gettysburgfoundation.org) is, appropriately enough, $18.63.

SHOPPING
Downtown Gettysburg
You won't find the Gap or a Starbucks in downtown Gettysburg. Its shops are of the independent variety, and many offer things you'd be hard-pressed to find in a big city: Civil War collectibles, military artifacts from the American Revolutionary War and onwards,

and anything a reenactor could want, from candle lanterns to cavalry swords. Dale Gallon and Mort Kunstler, two of the nation's premier historical artists, each have eponymous galleries in town: the **Gallon Historical Art Gallery** (9 Steinwehr Ave., 717/334-8666, www.gallon.com, 10 A.M.–5 P.M. Mon.–Sat. and noon–3 P.M. Sun.) and the **MKunstler Gallery** (10 York St., 717/334-0513, www.mkunstlergallery.com, call for hours).

Greater Gettysburg

Pennsylvania's sales tax exemption on clothing lures many a Marylander to the **Outlet Shoppes at Gettysburg** (1863 Gettysburg Village Dr., Gettysburg, 717/337-9705, www.theoutletshoppesatgettysburg.com, 10 A.M.–9 P.M. Mon.–Sat., 10 A.M.–6 P.M. Sun.) at U.S. 15 and Baltimore Street (Route 97). Retailers include Liz Claiborne, Jones New York, Old Navy, Naturalizer, Nautica, and Izod. There's a 10-screen cinema (717/338-0101) and hotel on-site.

Five miles south of downtown Gettysburg on U.S. Business Route 15 south is the flagship store of The Boyds Collection Ltd., best known for its plush bears and resin figurines. Billing itself as the "World's Most Humongous Teddy Bear Store," **Boyd's Bear Country** (75 Cunningham Rd., Gettysburg, 866/367-8338, www.boydsbearcountry.com, 10 A.M.–6 P.M. daily) carries collectibles available nowhere else, including a top-hatted Abraham Lincoln bear. In addition to Boyds products, the store sells collectibles and home decor from Gund, Yankee Candle, and more than 20 other companies. The four-story red barn is as much a family-fun destination as it is a store. Inside is a free museum that tells the Boyds story, a portrait center, and the Boyds Super Duper Bear Factory, where visitors can make their own bean-filled animal friend. Kids can adopt a plush canine at the Pups 'n Pals Adoption Center or take home a swaddled bear cub from the Boyds Teddy Bear Nursery. There's a deli open daily and a buffet-style eatery open on weekends. There's even a Guest Relations Center with information about area attractions, hotels, and more.

The quiet, tree-lined borough of **New Oxford,** 10 miles east of Gettysburg on U.S. 30, is an antiquing mecca with more than 500 dealers. A partial list of dealers can be found at www.newoxfordantiques.com, website of the New Oxford Antique Dealers Association.

SPORTS AND RECREATION

About 20 minutes from Gettysburg, **Liberty Mountain Resort** (78 Country Club Trail, Carroll Valley, 717/642-8282, www.skiliberty.com, 8-hour lift ticket $47–58, children 6–12 $42–52, ski rental $38, snowboard rental $44, snow tubing 1-hour session $15–20) offers skiing, snowboarding, and snow tubing when weather permits. A sister resort of York County's Ski Roundtop, Liberty Mountain has 16 trails, three terrain parks, and a 500-foot half-pipe. Skiers and snowboarders can choose from all-day, two-day, nighttime, and "flex" lift tickets good for four or eight hours from the time of purchase. Rossignol skis and Burton snowboards are available for rent. **Boulder Ridge Snow Tubing,** on the backside of the mountain, boasts more than a dozen lanes. One- and two-hour tickets are available for tubing sessions, which begin at the top of each hour. Kids 2–4 can tube all day in an area set aside for them for $9. The slopeside Liberty Mountain Hotel has 40 rooms ($125–149) and a suite with a kitchenette and hot tub ($189–209). Guests get free wireless Internet access and breakfast. Child care is available at $14–16 per hour. There's championship golfing next door to Liberty Mountain at **Carroll Valley Resort** (121 Sanders Rd., Fairfield, 717/642-8211, www.carrollvalley.com, accommodations $119–169).

ACCOMMODATIONS

Gettysburg has loads of lodging properties, many of which have a story to tell. There are B&Bs scarred by bullets and rooms once occupied by generals. You can unwind in a place that once crawled with wounded soldiers. If you visit when the town is crawling with tourists, expect two- or three-night minimums at many properties. Rates are at their lowest from December through March.

Under $100

Camping is a popular and inexpensive way to stay near the battlefield during the high season. Gettysburg has half a dozen campgrounds. If your idea of camping is quietly communing with nature with nothing but critters for company, you may be in for a shock. These campgrounds are fairly bustling places. Some have cottages so luxurious they make hotel rooms look rustic, and all offer a host of modern amenities. **Drummer Boy Camping Resort** (1300 Hanover St., Gettysburg, 800/293-2808, www.drummerboycampresort.com, tent sites $32–53 per night or $179–199 weekly, hookup sites $36–69 per night or $224–296 weekly, cabins $55–135 per night or $349–560 weekly, cottages $145–275 per night or $835–1,395 weekly) has, in addition to more than 400 campsites and about 50 cabins and cottages, two heated pools, a 250-foot water slide, a mini golf course, a game room, basketball and volleyball courts, and a pond where campers can fish without a license. Add to that a full schedule of activities and it's a wonder that campers ever leave the 95-acre resort. Drummer Boy is a few minutes east of downtown on Route 116.

A few minutes west of downtown on 116 is the 260-site **Gettysburg Campground** (2030 Fairfield Rd./Rte 116 W., Gettysburg, 717/334-3304, www.gettysburgcampground.com, tent sites $30–38 per night or $180–198 weekly, hookup sites $37–52 per night or $222–276 weekly, cabins $58–75 per night or $348–390 weekly, cottages $120–155 per night or $720–810 weekly). It too has amenities up the wazoo. Try to snag a campsite along Marsh Creek.

$100-200

Gettysburg's most iconic hotel, the ◖ **Best Western Gettysburg Hotel** (1 Lincoln Square, Gettysburg, 717/337-2000, www.hotelgettysburg.com, peak season $138–390, winter $100–250), is said to have a friendly ghost. You may or may not encounter the civil war nurse and wandering soul named Rachel during your stay. You'll definitely encounter friendly staff. The hotel in the center of town, just steps from the house where President Lincoln polished his

Gettysburg Address, is steeped in history. Its story begins in 1797, when a tavern opened its doors on the site. It withstood the bloody and pivotal battle of 1863 but was replaced in the 1890s by the current structure, which was christened the Hotel Gettysburg. In 1955 the hotel served as President Eisenhower's national operations center while he recuperated from a heart attack at his Gettysburg home. Eisenhower and his wife were the hotel's last guests before it closed its doors in 1964, rendered unprofitable by changes in travel habits. Ravaged by fire in 1983, the building was painstakingly restored and opened as a Best Western in 1991, grand as it ever was. The hotel has 119 guest accommodations, almost half of which are suites; a rooftop swimming pool; a fine dining restaurant open for breakfast and dinner; and an English-style pub with a mahogany bar shipped from across the pond. Check the website for a list of packages that bundle accommodations with activities such as skiing and theater-going.

Also historic but considerably smaller, the **James Gettys Hotel** (27 Chambersburg St., Gettysburg, 717/337-1334, www.jamesgettyshotel.com, $140–250) is half a block from the town square. Named for the founder of Gettysburg, it dates to 1804 and looks much as it did in the 1920s. Like the Gettysburg Hotel, it closed in the 1960s and reopened as an emulation of its former self in the 1990s. The James Gettys has a dozen suites, each with a bedroom, sitting room, kitchenette, and private bath. A complimentary continental breakfast is delivered to the suites daily. Housekeeping has been known to leave behind dark chocolates in the shape of the hotel.

With more than 300 guest rooms and suites, the **Eisenhower Hotel** (2634 Emmitsburg Rd., Gettysburg, 717/334-8121, www.eisenhower.com, $119–149) is the largest hotel in the area. Amenities include an indoor pool and Jacuzzi, a fitness room, dry saunas, a casual eatery, and a business center. A fun park on the hotel grounds features two go-kart tracks, 36 holes of miniature golf, a 14-acre fishing lake, and batting cages. Downtown Gettysburg is five miles to the north and the battlefield even closer.

B&B options in downtown Gettysburg include the impeccable **❰❰ Brickhouse Inn Bed & Breakfast** (452 Baltimore St., Gettysburg, 717/338-9337, www.brickhouseinn.com, $115–184). The older of its two buildings dates to the 1830s and was occupied by Confederate sharpshooters during the Battle of Gettysburg. Its south wall still bears the scars of Union bullets. The main house is an 1898 Victorian with original wood floors and chestnut trim. Between them they have 14 guest rooms and suites, each named for a state represented in the bloody battle. Breakfast always includes a hot entrée and the B&B's signature shoo-fly pie. Proprietors Tessa Bardo and Brian Duncan will give you the shirts off their backs but not the secret family recipe.

The **Brafferton Inn** (44 York St., Gettysburg, 717/337-3423, www.brafferton .com, $129–219) is another excellent choice. It has 18 uniquely decorated guest rooms and suites in four buildings—including the oldest deeded house in Gettysburg. The Brafferton is so centrally located—just half a block from the town square—that it can't offer private parking to all guests. Metered street parking is free 8 P.M.–8 A.M. and all day Sunday. Parking is also available in a municipal garage that charges 50 cents per hour.

The **Gaslight Inn** (33 E. Middle St., Gettysburg, 717/337-9100, www.thegaslight inn.com, $115–170) is yet another "in-town oasis," as innkeepers Mike and Betty Hanson put it. Their 1872 house has nine guest rooms, some of which boast Jacuzzis or steam baths, and a pair of furry residents: a Yorkie and a Pomeranian.

A few miles south of town is a countryside oasis, the **Lightner Farmhouse Bed & Breakfast** (2350 Baltimore Pike, Gettysburg, 717/337-9508, www.lightnerfarmhouse.com, $139–189). Built shortly before the Battle of Gettysburg, the Federal-style farmhouse was used as a hospital for three weeks after the bloodshed. Nothing gory about the place today. Innkeepers Dennis and Eileen Hoover aim to provide "outrageous service," whether preparing breakfast or arranging a crash course

in paranormal investigation. The B&B has five en suite rooms, a suite that sleeps up to four, and a two-floor cottage with a private wraparound deck. Quilt designs inspired their decor. Nature trails wind through the 19-acre property.

Built circa 1797, the **Cashtown Inn** (1325 Old Rte. 30, Cashtown, 717/334-9722, www .cashtowninn.com, $140–185) was the first stagecoach stop west of Gettysburg. It owes its name to its original innkeeper, who accepted only cash, and gave its name to the village it calls home. These days, credit cards are welcome at the inn, which is known as much for its cuisine as its cozy accommodations. Its four rooms and three suites are named for Confederate generals, some of whom made their headquarters there during the summer of 1863. More recent (and welcome) guests have included actor Sam Elliott, who bunked there while filming the 1993 movie *Gettysburg,* and paranormal investigator Jason Hawes, who featured the Cashtown in an episode of his Syfy series, *Ghost Hunters.* Room rates include breakfast.

FOOD

Gettysburg is no dining mecca, but it offers a rare opportunity for culinary time travel. A number of restaurants specialize in period fare. Best of the bunch: the **Dobbin House Tavern** (89 Steinwehr Ave., Gettysburg, 717/334-2100, www.dobbinhouse.com), offering colonial and continental cuisine in Gettysburg's oldest building. The Dobbin House was built in 1776—the same year the American colonies declared their independence from Great Britain—as a home for an Irish-born minister and his large brood. It served as a station on the Underground Railroad in the mid-1800s and as a hospital in the immediate aftermath of the Battle of Gettysburg. Great pains have been taken to restore the house-turned-restaurant to its 18th-century appearance. Many of the antique furnishings match descriptions in the inventory of the minister's estate. The china and flatware match fragments unearthed during an excavation of the cellar. For casual dining, head to the basement Springhouse Tavern (open daily from 11:30 A.M., $8–25). With three natural springs and two fireplaces, it's a cozy and romantic spot (that can be clammy in winter and humid in summer). Specials include spit-roasted chicken, chargrilled strip steak, and barbecued ribs, all served with a hearth-baked roll. Fine dining is available in six candlelit rooms known as the Alexander Dobbin Dining Rooms (open daily from 5 P.M., $19–37). The "bedroom" features a table beneath a lace bed canopy. Servers in period attire help satisfy the craving for history that brings most visitors to Gettysburg. Reservations are accepted for the dining rooms but not the tavern, where you can expect a considerable wait on summer weekends.

The **Farnsworth House Inn** (401 Baltimore St., Gettysburg, 717/334-8838, www.farns worthhouseinn.com, dining rooms 5–9 P.M. daily, call for winter hours, $18–25) is another popular destination for period dining complete with costumed servers. Game pie, the house specialty, is a stew of turkey, pheasant, and duck topped with a golden egg crust. Built in the early 1800s, the house sheltered Confederate

sharpshooters during the Battle of Gettysburg. It's believed that one of the Southerners accidentally shot Jennie Wade, the only civilian killed during the three-day struggle. Oil paintings of the commanding officers at Gettysburg and photos by famed Civil War photographer Mathew Brady decorate the bullet-scarred house, which has been restored to its 1863 appearance. Its tavern (11:30 A.M.–10 P.M. daily, call for winter hours, $8–12), popular with reenactors, offers hot and cold sandwiches, pork and sauerkraut, meatloaf, and more. Garden dining is available in the warmer months.

Eight miles west of Gettysburg on Route 116, the **Fairfield Inn** (15 W. Main St., Gettysburg, 717/642-5410, www.thefairfieldinn.com, lunch 11 A.M.–4 P.M. Fri.–Sat., brunch 11 A.M.–3 P.M. Sun., dinner 5–9 P.M. Tues.–Sat. and 3–8 P.M. Sun., lunch $6–12, dinner $17–32) has hosted such VIPs as Thaddeus Stevens and President Dwight D. Eisenhower since opening in 1757. The day after the Battle of Gettysburg, as the weary Confederate army retreated west through Fairfield, the inn hosted their generals. Today's guests can sup on hearty ham and

the Farnsworth House Inn

bean soup and chicken and biscuits, just like General Robert E. Lee, or choose from dishes like Tuscan penne, fried haddock, and roasted half duck with balsamic fig reduction. Sunday brunch ($18 per person, children 5–12 $7) is a three-course affair.

If you're not into period dining, you're not out of luck. The Gettysburg area has some recommendable restaurants that go a different route. **Gettysburg Eddie's** (217 Steinwehr Ave., Gettysburg, 717/334-1100, www.gettys burgeddies.com, 11 A.M.–10 P.M. Sun.–Thurs., 11 A.M.–10:30 P.M. Fri.–Sat., bar open until 11 P.M. Sun.–Thurs. and midnight Fri.–Sat., call for winter hours, $8–27), across the street from Soldiers' National Cemetery, is a casual, welcoming spot with a stamp of approval from the sustainability-promoting Green Restaurant Association. Named for Baseball Hall of Fame pitcher Eddie Plank, born in 1875 on a farm north of Gettysburg, the restaurant has an expansive menu that includes foot-long franks, steaks (cut in house daily), sizzling fajitas, and pasta dishes. The house-made peanut butter pie is a home run. Big LCD TVs and a full-service bar make Eddie's a popular place to watch college and pro sports.

Herr Tavern & Publick House (900 Chambersburg Rd., Gettysburg, 717/334-4332, www.herrtavern.com, lunch 11 A.M.–3 P.M. Wed.–Fri. and 11:30 A.M.–3 P.M. Sat., dinner 5–9 P.M. daily, lunch $8–13, dinner $24–34) is an excellent choice for fine dining. Servers are happy to talk guests through the creative menu, which changes weekly, and extensive wine list, a winner of *Wine Enthusiast Magazine*'s Unique Distinction Award. Built in 1815, the tavern was turned into a Confederate hospital during the 1863 clash of armies. It's said that amputated limbs were thrown out of a window into a waiting wagon. Given the gruesomeness of what went down, it's no wonder the staff have some ghost stories to share. Herr Tavern is just west of downtown Gettysburg on U.S. 30. A few miles farther west is another historic and reportedly haunted dining destination. The (**Cashtown Inn** (1325 Old Rte. 30, Cashtown, 717/334-9722, www .cashtowninn.com, lunch 11:30 A.M.–2 P.M. and dinner 5 P.M. Tues.–Sat., lunch $6–14, dinner

the Cashtown Inn

$19–32) was also overrun by Confederates during the battle. The general who assumed command of the defeated army's retreat made it his headquarters. Its current owners have resisted the temptation to lure history-hungry tourists with period fare, offering New American cuisine instead. They rely on local farmers and producers for everything from eggs and apples to wines and beers.

If you don't mind a bit of a drive, head to the **Altland House** (Center Square, Abbottstown, 717/259-9535, www.altlandhouse.com), a hotel about midway between Gettysburg and York on U.S. 30. Its main restaurant, **Lulu's Grille and Spirits** (11 A.M.–8 P.M. Tues., 11 A.M.–9 P.M. Wed.–Sat., 11 A.M.–8 P.M. Sun., lunch $7–17, dinner $10–28), is a popular spot for celebrating anniversaries and other special occasions. "Trends" (as in the chef's latest creations) share the menu with "traditions" (as in chicken and crab casserole and meatloaf with red-skinned mashed potatoes). The hotel's **Underside Pub and Eatery** (5–11 P.M. Wed.–Sat., $8–28) offers a more casual setting and live entertainment most Friday and Saturday evenings. You can order off the pub menu at Lulu's and vice versa.

INFORMATION

Visit the website of the **Gettysburg Convention & Visitors Bureau** (717/334-6274, www.gettysburg.travel) to request a free copy of its official visitors guide or peruse a digital version. The CVB operates information desks in the Gettysburg National Military Park Museum and Visitor Center and the David Wills House. For information about Pennsylvania Dutch Country as a whole, visit www.dutchcountryroads.com.

GETTING THERE AND AROUND

Gettysburg is in the center of Adams County, which hugs the Pennsylvania-Maryland line just west of York County. The town is about 40 miles southwest of Harrisburg and 60 miles northwest of Baltimore. **Harrisburg International Airport** (888/235-9442, www.flyhia.com) is served by Air Canada, AirTran Airways, Continental Airlines, Delta Air Lines, United Airlines, and US Airways. They offer daily nonstop service to about a dozen destinations. Note that while locals refer to the airport as HIA, its Federal Aviation Administration booking code is MDT. That's because of its physical location in the borough of Middletown, about eight miles south of Harrisburg. The larger **Baltimore/Washington International Thurgood Marshall Airport** (800/435-9294, www.bwiairport.com) is served by about 25 commercial airlines. Private aircraft can fly into **Gettysburg Regional Airport** (www.flyhia.com) just west of town.

There's no passenger train or commercial bus service into Gettysburg. It's very much a driving destination. Public transportation within Gettysburg debuted in 2009. **Freedom Transit** (717/845-7433, www.ridethetrolley.com) operates trolley-like buses on three fixed routes. The tourist-oriented route, named the Lincoln Line, connects downtown Gettysburg and Gettysburg National Military Park. Lincoln Line service is available 8 A.M.–10 P.M. daily April–November and on a more limited basis in the winter. The cash fare is $1, and transfers are free. An all-day pass is $3 and can be purchased on Freedom Transit's website. Ten-ride and monthly passes are also available. Seniors and children 5 and under ride for free.

www.moon.com

MOON.COM is ready to help plan your next trip! Filled with fresh trip ideas and strategies, author interviews, informative travel blogs, a detailed map library, and descriptions of all the Moon guidebooks, Moon.com is all you need to get out and explore the world—or even places in your own backyard. While at Moon.com, sign up for our monthly e-newsletter for updates on new releases, travel tips, and expert advice from our on-the-go Moon authors. As always, when you travel with Moon, expect an experience that is uncommon and truly unique.

MOON IS ON FACEBOOK—BECOME A FAN!
JOIN THE MOON PHOTO GROUP ON FLICKR

MAP SYMBOLS

▤▤▤ Expressway	◖ Highlight	✗ Airfield	⚓ Golf Course	
▦▦▦ Primary Road	○ City/Town	✈ Airport	₽ Parking Area	
─── Secondary Road	◉ State Capital	▲ Mountain	◀ Archaeological Site	
▫▫▫ Unpaved Road	⊛ National Capital	✚ Unique Natural Feature	♠ Church	
------ Trail	★ Point of Interest		🜚 Gas Station	
·········· Ferry	• Accommodation	⚑ Waterfall	Glacier	
━•━•━ Railroad	▼ Restaurant/Bar	▲ Park	Mangrove	
▨▨▨ Pedestrian Walkway	■ Other Location	❶ Trailhead	Reef	
▥▥▥ Stairs	Λ Campground	⚐ Skiing Area	Swamp	

CONVERSION TABLES

°C = (°F - 32) / 1.8
°F = (°C x 1.8) + 32
1 inch = 2.54 centimeters (cm)
1 foot = 0.304 meters (m)
1 yard = 0.914 meters
1 mile = 1.6093 kilometers (km)
1 km = 0.6214 miles
1 fathom = 1.8288 m
1 chain = 20.1168 m
1 furlong = 201.168 m
1 acre = 0.4047 hectares
1 sq km = 100 hectares
1 sq mile = 2.59 square km
1 ounce = 28.35 grams
1 pound = 0.4536 kilograms
1 short ton = 0.90718 metric ton
1 short ton = 2,000 pounds
1 long ton = 1.016 metric tons
1 long ton = 2,240 pounds
1 metric ton = 1,000 kilograms
1 quart = 0.94635 liters
1 US gallon = 3.7854 liters
1 Imperial gallon = 4.5459 liters
1 nautical mile = 1.852 km

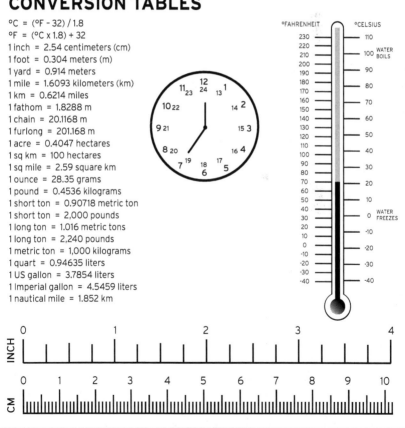

MOON SPOTLIGHT PENNSYLVANIA DUTCH COUNTRY

Avalon Travel
a member of the Perseus Books Group
1700 Fourth Street
Berkeley, CA 94710, USA
www.moon.com

Editor: Shaharazade Husain
Series Manager: Kathryn Ettinger
Copy Editor: Naomi Adler Dancis
Graphics and Production Coordinator:
  Elizabeth Jang
Cover Designer: Kathryn Osgood
Map Editor: Brice Ticen
Cartographer: Kat Bennett

ISBN: 978-1-59880-827-8

ABOUT THE AUTHOR

Anna Dubrovsky

Anna Dubrovsky has lived in more than a dozen cities on three continents and has explored countless others. She has wandered through the Louvre in Paris and the Hermitage in St. Petersburg, Russia, where she was born; she has cycled the western coast of Ireland, hang-glided over Rio, motorcycled up a mountain in the Dominican Republic, scuba-dived in Costa Rica, and camped along the Appalachian Trail; she has marveled at the Taj Mahal, prayed at the Western Wall, and danced in Havana. Yet she still keeps coming back to Pennsylvania.

Anna first set foot in the Keystone State when her 7th-grade class ventured from Cleveland to Philadelphia, belting Whitney Houston ballads all the way. Her family relocated to Pittsburgh a couple of years later, and Anna's first driver's license was a Pennsylvania one. After her sophomore year at Northwestern University, she returned to Pennsylvania for a reporting internship at *The Morning Call* of Allentown, where she covered The Great Allentown Fair from the perspective of a sheep. She interned at the *Pittsburgh Post-Gazette* after her junior year and worked as a statehouse reporter for the *York Daily Record* after graduating. In 1999 she left the newspaper and Pennsylvania for New York City, where she covered City Hall for an online news service.

After stints as a financial reporter in New Jersey and Los Angeles and as a student of yoga in India, Anna followed her heart back to Pittsburgh, bought a house and a membership to the world-class Carnegie Museums, and began a career as a freelance writer and yoga teacher. Finally, she has an answer to a question that has always stumped her: "Where are you from?"